EXPLORING CAREERS IN JOURNALISM

EXPLORING CAREERS
IN JOURNALISM

By

THOMAS PAWLICK

RICHARDS ROSEN PRESS, INC.
New York, N.Y. 10010

Published in 1981 by Richards Rosen Press, Inc.
29 East 21st Street, New York, N.Y. 10010

Copyright 1981 by Thomas Pawlick

First Edition

Library of Congress Cataloging in Publication Data

Pawlick, Thomas.
  Exploring careers in journalism.

  (Careers in depth)
  SUMMARY: Presents an overview of the news
industry and discusses how to prepare for and get a
job in journalism.
    1. Journalism—Vocational guidance. [1. Journalism
—Vocational guidance. 2. Vocational guidance]
I. Title.
PN4797.P35   070′.23′73   80–36782
ISBN 0–8239–0515–2

Manufactured in the United States of America

To JOANNE

About the Author

Thomas Pawlick is a veteran journalist with more than 15 years' experience writing and editing for newspapers, magazines, and wire services in the United States and Canada. Born in Detroit, Michigan, in 1941, he studied at Michigan State University; the Université de Poitiers, France; Marygrove College, and at the University of Detroit, from which he received a bachelor of arts degree in 1965. He has worked as a reporter or an editor for the Detroit *News,* the Associated Press, Michigan's Booth Newspapers chain, and the Montreal *Gazette* and is presently employed as an associate editor of *Harrowsmith Magazine.* In 1974 he was awarded the Canadian Science Writers Association National Journalism Award, and in 1975 he received the U.S. National Conference of Christians and Jews Brotherhood Award for Journalism. His poetry and free-lance articles have appeared in publications throughout the U.S. and Canada, including the Chicago *Sun-Times,* Detroit *Free Press,* Montreal *Star,* the *Chicago Journalism Review,* and *Canadian Forum,* as well as in numerous literary magazines. A former high school teacher, he served for two years as training editor of the Montreal *Gazette,* responsible for the organization and implementation of the paper's intern program for journalism students. One of his students subsequently won the National Newspaper Award, Canada's highest journalism award, and a second received the Roland Michener Award for public service in journalism. Mr. Pawlick is married to the former Joanne Wolk and lives with her and their three children on a small farm in rural Canada.

Preface

The craft of journalism is an exciting and often highly rewarding profession that combines personal satisfaction and creativity with the opportunity to perform a real public service for a community—keeping the people informed.

Unfortunately, myths and tall tales about the newspaper business and broadcasting abound, giving those who might be well fitted for such work a confused, distorted picture of what newsmen and women really do and why they do it.

Many young men and women, particularly those who have innate writing talent, would like to work as journalists but have no idea how they might go about breaking into the profession. Some, lacking information, assume that such a career is beyond their reach.

This book is intended to destroy some of the myths about journalists and their work and to provide interested persons with a realistic overview of the news industry—an industry in which they may well find a place.

The opinions presented are, of course, personal, and not everyone will agree with them. They have, however, the saving grace of being based on several years of direct experience in nearly every aspect of the business. They are the informed opinion of someone who has been there. Hopefully, they will prove useful to others.

THOMAS PAWLICK

Contents

I.	*The Industry*	3
II.	*"I Love This Crazy Business"*	18
III.	*Why News People Go Gray*	30
IV.	*What Managing Editors Want*	43
V.	*Schools and Schools of Hard Knocks*	52
VI.	*Your Foot in the Door*	64
VII.	*On the Job*	75
VIII.	*Continuing Your Education*	87
IX.	*Many and Various*	97
X.	*Read On . . .*	106
	Appendix	112

EXPLORING CAREERS IN JOURNALISM

CHAPTER I

The Industry

Anyone taking bets on the future of journalism in North America when the continent's first newspaper was published in 1690 would have been justified in not giving the industry very long odds on survival. Politicians in those days did not like the idea of ordinary citizens poking their noses into government affairs, much less writing about them, and Boston printer Benjamin Harris' paper, *Publick Occurrences Both Forreign and Domestick,* was shut down by the governor of Massachusetts immediately after putting out its first—and only—issue.

Fortunately, Harris wasn't the only printer brave enough to challenge the censors of his day. Despite the knuckle-rap administered to him, other men, including Benjamin Franklin's older brother, James, soon followed his example by bringing out papers of their own, and the industry grew like a weed.

Today, its branches and shoots are a luxuriant growth, penetrating every corner of society in the United States and Canada. There are thousands of newspapers, magazines, and radio and television stations, representing an endless variety of opinion. Their sheer numbers, at first glance, would seem enough to bewilder any attempt to catalog or classify them.

Basically, however, journalism in North America can be divided into six categories: 1) the daily press; 2) the wire services; 3) weekly newspapers; 4) the trade press; 5) general magazines; and 6) broadcast journalism. Each category has its own peculiarities and, for the job-seeker, its own advantages and drawbacks.

For example, the reporters and editors who work for large metropolitan daily newspapers or the wire services are usually well paid. If they are fortunate enough to belong to a union, such as the North American Newspaper Guild or the Wire Service Guild, they may also enjoy a high degree of job security. But getting a job with a wire service or a major daily newspaper can be extremely difficult. Because the rewards of such jobs are substantial, the competition for them is fierce.

The reporters and editors who work for weekly newspapers or the trade press, on the other hand, generally earn lower salaries than their counterparts in the "big time" and enjoy less job security. But access to jobs in these two areas is much easier for the beginner, and working for such publications can provide the kind of experience that may lead to later advancement.

The Daily Press

The daily press, which includes all of the daily newspapers published across the continent, is the backbone of the industry. It includes major papers like the Chicago *Sun Times* with a circulation of more than 550,000 readers, and smaller ones like the Menominee (Mich.) *Herald-Leader* with a circulation of 4,500.

At one time most of the dailies in North America were independently owned by publishers located in the cities where they appeared. Today, however, ownership has become concentrated, and the majority of dailies are owned by large corporate chains or newspaper groups that publish newspapers in several cities.

Both the Detroit *Free Press* and the Miami *Herald,* for example, belong to the Knight Newspapers group, and in Canada both the Montreal *Gazette* and the Vancouver *Province* are owned by Southam Newspapers.

Some newspaper chains, like the Gannett group, are huge. They may include fifty or more papers in as many cities, and some industry critics have charged that the big chains are monopolies. In recent years, antitrust suits have been launched in the United States against corporations that own radio or television stations in the same cities as their daily papers. The antitrust lawyers have contended that such blanket ownership of all of the communications media in a single city stifles free speech.

In practice, however, most chains allow their member papers or stations a relatively large measure of editorial independence. The control the head office exercises is focused more on the financial side of a paper's operation than on its news content.

Many newspaper chains form syndicates for the distribution of news stories, columns, and feature articles to all of the member papers in the chain. Southam Newspapers, for example, has the Southam Press subsidiary, which employs its own staff of special writers in Washington, D.C., Ottawa, and London, England.

Most individual daily newspapers cannot afford the expense of maintaining staff members in various cities. They have their hands full just covering their own circulation area. Belonging to a chain with its own syndicate network, however, enables them to obtain news from other cities and other countries without having to send their own reporters there.

News from other cities and countries is also obtained through the wire services, such as the Associated Press, United Press International, the Canadian Press, Reuters, and Agence France Press.

The Wire Services

Virtually every daily newspaper and many weekly papers subscribe to one or more of the wire services. The corner of almost every newsroom contains either a bank of old-style electric teleprinters that click out stories from around the world under the AP (Associated Press), UPI (United Press International), or some other logotype, or a computerized receiver/storage system with video display terminals, on which stories can be called up from the computer's "memory" and displayed on a lighted screen for editing. Papers equipped with the latter system have machines in the "back shop," or printers' area, which automatically set wire service stories in type as they come pulsing through the electronic circuits.

The stories thus received are part of the basic product each wire service provides for its subscribers for a set monthly fee. Usually the service also includes electronically transmitted "wire photos," which also come in on special machines.

The Associated Press, which is the largest of the wire services, is a cooperative, literally owned by all its member papers, who are shareholders in the firm. Most of the other wire services are privately owned enterprises. The larger wire services function twenty-four hours a day, in shifts. Their computers and teleprinters never stop running. As the AP motto says, they have a "deadline every minute," and the competition among them is strong. Each service keeps a running score of the number of papers that use its version of a story, rather than a competing service's version, and woe betide the local bureau that is consistently outclassed by its rivals. Heads roll.

Wire services maintain bureaus in most of the major cities of the world, from San Francisco to Hong Kong. Because the subscriber papers they serve represent a wide variety of political and social opinion, the wire services cannot afford to write slanted or biased stories. What might please a conservative Republican subscriber in Illinois may offend a liberal Democratic editor in New York.

For reporters, the knowledge that they will be permitted to write the objective facts, without bias, while working for a wire service is an attractive point. All too often, working for an individual newspaper, they lack editorial freedom and are forced to toe the publisher's line.

The larger measure of editorial freedom provided in wire service writing, however, is often offset by the restrictions on writing style it poses. A colorful piece of personal interpretation of a news event is difficult to produce when every word is weighed to be sure no bias intrudes. Also overshadowing the writer's freedom is the frequently heavy work load. A good deal of an AP or UPI writer's output consists of rewrites from local papers, sometimes twenty-five or thirty stories per shift. Wire service people, on average, work twice as hard as their counterparts on daily newspapers, and usually twice as fast.

Weekly Newspapers

The weekly paper is to the newspaper industry what a precinct delegate is to a political party: it is the grassroots. While wire services and daily papers deal with the "big" stories, citywide, national, and international news, the weekly's focus is more modest. It deals with the neighborhood, the suburb or the small town, with the fate of Central High School's baseball team rather than the exploits of the major-league pennant contenders.

It deals, in other words, with the basic nuts and bolts of a community, the doings of the local zoning board or school board representative. Writing for a weekly may not be glamorous, but it can provide opportunities for genuine public service and the immediate satisfaction of having your next-door neighbor's best interests in hand.

Unfortunately, just as writing for a weekly paper affords the chance for direct service to a community, it also risks drawing direct pressure from that community. Weekly papers are more vulnerable than dailies to pressure from local advertisers or groups of citizens. In some communities the editor of the local weekly feels as if he's walking on eggs. A northern Michigan weekly, for example, was put out of business in the mid-1960's when a story it ran offended local merchants. They boycotted the paper and, with no advertising revenue, it folded.

Reporters on weekly papers also have heavy work loads and frequently act as jacks-of-all-trades, doing photography and some printing as well as writing stories and selling advertisements.

The Trade Press

The trade press includes those newspapers that are published, daily or weekly, to serve a particular industry, trade, or profession. *Stamp News,* for example, serves stamp dealers as well as individual stamp collectors. *Labor News* reports on the union movement, and *Pulp and Paper News* covers the paper pulp industry.

Such publications are highly specialized, and those who write for them must limit their scope to include only that subject in which the paper's readers have a professional concern. Although writing for a trade publication is limiting, jobs in this area are generally easier to come by than in the daily press. Few aspiring reporters consider the trade press as a possibility when they start job-hunting, and consequently the field has fewer competitors.

Clippings of articles written for trade papers also make good samples to show the editor of a larger paper when you ask him for a job. They prove you've gotten your feet wet in the business and know how to write clear, concise stories.

The trade press may also include magazines and newsletters written by employees of corporations for their fellow staff members. For example, Michigan Consolidated Gas Corporation publishes a newsletter, *The Pilot Light,* and a magazine, *The Gasette,* for its employees. Such publications are also good training grounds for reporters breaking into the business. Many corporate "in-house" publications, however, are really public relations vehicles rather than news organs, and thus are considered part of the public relations profession rather than that of journalism.

General Magazines

Except for television broadcasters, who may earn more money, magazine writers are generally the envy of their fellow journalists. Writing for a nationally known magazine, from *Time* and *Newsweek* to *Harper's, Outdoor Life,* or *The Ladies' Home Journal,* is considered a prestige job, the top of the heap. The only way to rise higher than such a job is to write a best-selling book, sell it to Hollywood, and retire to live off your royalties.

Most of the writers for such magazines have put in years of apprenticeship on newspapers or as free-lance writers before they got a full-time job with their present employer. Even an experienced news writer would consider himself lucky to sell a single free-lance article to *Harper's* or *Esquire,* let alone find a full-time job on the magazine's regular staff. Such publications are exceptionally unlikely places for a beginner to find a job.

There is, however, an endless variety of local and specialized magazines where a beginner has an even chance not only of selling free-lance articles, but of finding full-time work as well. Just as there are trade papers, there are also trade magazines, which cater to everything from antique car buffs to ski bums and rabbit farmers. Many of these specialized magazines are of high quality, and working for them can mean a higher salary than that earned on most weekly newspapers.

Broadcast Journalism

Broadcast journalism includes both radio and television and has become an industry in itself, worthy of a separate book. Radio is its grassroots, as well as the area most likely to offer the beginner work. Virtually every city and town has at least one AM radio station, and many university campuses have student-run radio stations of their own where the neophyte can gain practical experience.

Television is the big time, with big salaries, and quite difficult to break into without prior experience in some other form of journalism.

Most of the major wire services maintain separate wires for broadcast news, and those who provide the copy for the broadcast wire write in a different style from those handling copy for newspaper subscribers. News "splits," the short digests of major headlines read every half hour by radio news announcers, are measured in seconds, rather than lines or paragraphs—the number of seconds it takes an announcer to read them aloud into the microphone.

The Alternative Press

In the 1960's and early 1970's a vast number of so-called underground and alternative newspapers and magazines sprang into being, focusing their reporting on issues involving the Vietnam War, the black civil rights movement, the back-to-the-land movement, Women's Liberation, and the drug culture. Many of these publications were amateurish, sloppily written, and biased to the point of nausea, but some were excellent, providing insights and opinions not covered in the so-called establishment press.

Since the end of the Vietnam War and the downfall of former President Richard M. Nixon, most of the poorer-quality, purely political undergrounds have disappeared, but a few of the better alternative publications, such as *The Village Voice* and *Rolling Stone,* have survived. Their writing has become more objective, but they still tend to place themselves on the cutting edge of change in society.

Other "counter-cultural" publications, like *Mother Earth News* in the U.S. and Canada's *Harrowsmith Magazine,* focus on the back-to-the-land movement, alternative energy use such as solar or wind power, and the changing rural scene. Some, like *Mother Jones,* concentrate on investigative reporting. *Harrowsmith* also does an occasional investigative story, usually with a rural setting.

The quality of such publications has become so high that they can be considered part of the established scene in journalism, but their approach is generally fresh and innovative.

It Takes All Kinds

At any newspaper, magazine, or broadcast outlet, there is a wide variety of jobs to be done. Writing an article or broadcast script is only one of them. A major daily newspaper, for example, may employ more than 200 people in as many different kinds of jobs. There are printers, photographers, telephone operators, advertising salesmen, security guards, and stenographers.

All of them are essential to the production of the newspaper, but it is the editorial division, made up of writers, editors, and photographers, that provides the paper's basic product: the news, and views, of the community and the world.

At the top of the heap is the publisher, who either owns or manages the paper. Under him is the editor in chief or the managing editor, who supervises the whole editorial department, sometimes with the help of one or more assistant managing editors. Next in line are the news editor, who oversees publication of national stories and wire service copy; the city editor, who oversees the gathering and publication of

The mail room of a daily newspaper, including the conveyor-roller on which bundles of newspapers roll out to be sorted before going to the delivery trucks (photo by Thomas Pawlick).

local news; and the makeup editor, whose task is to decide where each story should appear in the paper and, somehow, to see that they all fit into the space available on the page.

Departments, such as sports, business, or entertainment, have their own editors. The editorial page, including the letters-to-the-editor column, also has its own editor, who usually oversees the newspaper's resident political cartoonist as well.

Next in the pecking order are the writers who produce regular columns for the paper, usually chosen for their colorful writing style and ability to produce original material on a daily basis. Often, columnists end up selling their work to several papers, establishing a national reputation and a regular "fan club" of readers. They frequently become local celebrities and the butt of numerous barbs from their envious fellow workers, who regard them as prima donnas.

The real foot soldiers of a newspaper, however, are the copy editors, reporters, and photographers who produce the majority of stories and pictures that fill every page. The copy editors are like an army's sergeants, the reporters and photographers its Pfc's, or, as the U.S. Marines say, "the grunts."

At most dailies an assignment editor, who sometimes doubles as a copy editor, keeps track of the phone calls, anonymous tips, news releases, and editions of rival papers that come into the newsroom every day. When he decides a story should be covered, he picks a reporter and photographer to do the job. The reporter and photographer go to the scene of the news event, interview those involved, take pictures, then return and put together a story.

The reporter's story then goes to the copy editors, who sit around

A photo editor sizes a picture before it is processed for reproduction (photo by Thomas Pawlick).

a big desk called "the rim." There it is read for errors of fact, spelling, grammar, or style. It is corrected or rewritten, and a suitable headline is written for it. In the past, reporters typed their stories on ordinary typewriters, and the copy editors corrected them in pencil, usually a pencil with blue lead. The term "blue pencil," used as a verb, is still synonymous in newsrooms with "correct" or "delete." In recent years, however, the process of writing and editing copy has been computerized. Stories are composed and corrected on video display terminals, nicknamed VDT's, connected directly to typesetting machines in the back shop. The copy is displayed electronically on a screen as it is typed on the computer keyboard, rather than on paper. While all this is being done, the photographer's developed prints go to the photo editor and then to the makeup editor, who makes the initial decisions on how to "play" stories and photos, that is, where to put them on the page.

The final decisions on story play are made in a daily editorial conference, usually chaired by the managing editor. Once the stories have been edited and given headlines, the photos developed and selected, and the pages laid out, everything goes to the back shop, where the paper's printers see to it that the edition rolls off the presses and onto the delivery trucks, headed for the readers.

The circulation department's delivery trucks keep a tight daily schedule, and to meet it the newspaper must get out on time. Each department has its own daily deadline, by which time stories and photos must be turned in. Anyone who cannot meet a deadline, or withstand the pressure to produce that it creates, will not last long in journalism. Among newspeople, deadlines are sacrosanct. As the saying goes: "The Second Coming of Christ won't get in the paper if it doesn't meet the deadline."

Years ago, many daily papers published four or more editions per day, competing fiercely with each edition to be the first to report an event and "scoop" their rivals. The task of meeting deadlines in those days was made easier by the presence of rewrite men. Reporters in the field, rather than take the time to return to the paper and write their stories themselves, would simply telephone the details in while a rewrite man took notes. The rewrite man would then write the story.

Today, the rapidity with which radio and television can relay bulletins of a news event has made the publishing of several newspaper editions per day unnecessary. As a result, reporters have more time to do their own writing and the rewrite man has all but disappeared. The last person to hold the rewrite job at the Detroit *Free Press,* for example, was James Dewey, a veteran journalist who died in 1979. Since his death his post has been left unfilled.

The rewrite man was generally the best writer on a newspaper's staff, able to assemble a clear, readable article from the breathless, sometimes garbled and fragmentary details his "legmen" phoned in, and to do so with often incredible speed. In the Golden Age of "scoop journalism," the rewrite man was king and idolized by cub reporters.

Unfortunately the age of the Big Scoop, from about 1920 to 1950, was also the age of newspaper sensationalism, of tabloids like the New York *Mirror* and the *Graphic,* which specialized in scandal, crime, and sex stories, in the doings of movie stars and the latest ax murder. The wild excesses of those who wrote the headlines for such papers were only outdone by the antics of their legmen and photographers, who would do just about anything short of commit murder themselves to get a splashy story.

This era of madness ended when the *National Enquirer,* by then already an anachronism, decided in the early 1960's to drop its sensationalistic format in favor of a more muted, responsible approach to the

An editor questions a reporter about a story in the newsroom of a daily paper.

news. The newspaper industry today is still trying to live down the unsavory reputation the old-time tabloids created for it.

Newspapers, of course, still try to scoop each other, and nothing gives an editor greater satisfaction than to scoop the arch rival, television. But the contest today is conducted at a slower, saner pace. Generally, if scooping a rival news organization would mean sacrificing accuracy, most papers pass up the opportunity.

Pounding the Beat

The reporters at most newspapers are divided into two groups, those with beats and those on general assignment. Beat reporters are assigned to cover specific subject areas, such as labor, city hall, or science news. Each has regular rounds to make and telephone contacts to run through each day and must keep abreast of events in his or her particular circle. As beat reporters are in constant contact with their sources, they usually hear of news events before the assignment editor does and often decide themselves whether a story should be covered or not.

Labor reporters, for example, eventually get to know the leaders of the union locals in their city on a personal basis, and many rank-and-file union members know the labor reporter by his or her first name. Police reporters become friendly with police officers—and sometimes with criminals—are invited to officers' homes for dinner, and hear all the latest gossip of the department.

The close friendships that often develop on the beat may prove an advantage in getting news, but they can also create personal dilemmas for reporters. It is difficult, for example, to report the story of a bribe scandal in the police department objectively if one of those involved happens to be a good friend of the reporter writing the story. Beat reporters must tread a thin line between loyalty to their friends and loyalty to their readership.

General assignment reporters, as their title indicates, do not have a special beat. They are the assignment editor's mobile corps, available to cover any event that does not fall in a regular beat reporter's territory, or to back up the beat reporter when he or she cannot cover a story alone. They never know, when they go to work in the morning, what kind of story they will be covering that day. It may be anything from a speech by the mayor, the sinking of a ship in the harbor, or a report on the weather to covering a riot, a five-alarm fire, or a heart transplant.

A general assignment reporter at the Montreal *Gazette,* for example, came to work one morning expecting to do a routine color story on the people and rides at a local amusement park. Instead, he found himself sent to the scene of a riot at a nearby plant where security guards had opened fire with shotguns on striking union members picketing outside the factory. One of the strikers, standing less than a yard away from the reporter, was gunned down by a shotgun blast while talking to newsmen.

Unlike the beat reporter, whose job can become somewhat routine, the general assignment reporter lives a life full of surprises.

Cub reporters who are new at the game are often put on general assignment because they have not had time to develop a specialty. Fre-

Two reporters at their desks, one using a typewriter, the other a computer terminal keyboard called the VDT or video display terminal (photo by Thomas Pawlick).

quently, however, a paper's best reporters, with the most experience and most colorful writing styles, are also on general assignment.

Some of them become "feature writers," whose stories focus less on a given news event than on the personalities involved in it and the deeper meanings behind it. Their stories, which often have permanent literary merit beyond the immediate moment, are written under deadline pressure just like everyone else's. Yet they strive to bring a different view of the news to the public, covering aspects of an event that cannot be conveyed in the conventional straight news account. The interpretations of some of the better feature writers are often as complex and as moving as the work of any novelist.

Women and Minorities

Twenty years ago the vast majority of reporters and editors were white, and almost every one of them was male. The few reporters who were female were generally assigned to the "Women's Pages," where they wrote stories on cooking, homemaking, or the doings of socialites. Black reporters were for the most part found only on the staffs of weekly papers serving the black community.

Today things have changed.

Nearly half of the reporting staff at many metropolitan dailies is made up of women, and female copy editors and department heads are no longer rarities. Female publishers and managing editors are still scarce, and on some papers women journalists still receive lower salaries than their male counterparts, but the days of male supremacy in journalism are definitely over. The battle for equal employment opportunities for women in journalism was not easy, and some skirmishes remain to be fought, but in the main the openings for advancement for female journalists are better now than at any time in history. They are far wider than in many other lines of work.

The racial bar against blacks, Spanish-speaking people, and other minority groups has also been broken at most large dailies.

Part of the reason for this change in hiring practices was simple embarrassment. Newspapers reporting stories on the black civil rights movement or Women's Liberation in the 1960's found it acutely difficult to editorialize in favor of fair employment when their own staffs were a glaring example of the opposite attitude.

Editors also found that it was easier for a black reporter to cover a sit-in or for a woman to cover a Women's Lib demonstration because

Three women reporters at work in a newspaper city room (photo by Thomas Pawlick).

those they were sent to interview did not look on them as the enemy, as representatives of an exploiting class. White male reporters often could not do an effective job because they could not gain their subjects' confidence.

A combination of uneasy consciences, the desire to provide adequate news coverage, and the insistent pressure brought by women and members of minority groups to force change together worked a sort of newsroom revolution. There are still some newspapers where this kind of change is resisted, but they are swimming against the current. Generally, the field of journalism is open to anyone with ability and determination, regardless of sex, race, or any other attribute.

CHAPTER II

"I Love This Crazy Business"

The city editor of the Montreal *Gazette,* Jim Peters, stood sipping rye and ginger at the bar of the Ottawa Press Club. Outside, the evening sky was gray and chilly, but inside the lights were mellow and the room was warm. The bar was half full of men and women of various ages, mostly newspaper people, television broadcasters, public relations men, and a scattering of the civil servants who worked in one or another of the government buildings that are spotted throughout Canada's national capital.

Their voices blended into a quiet buzz in the background. Individual conversations were difficult to make out, but the talk, as always in such places, was a mixture of gossip, tips on news events about to happen, political intrigue, secrets being leaked—or covered up—and tales of recent adventures shared or future actions planned. At a table in a corner, a reporter from Toronto was talking earnestly with a nervous-looking man in horn-rimmed glasses. Perhaps the nervous man was a government employee, risking his job to leak secret information about political corruption to the reporter. Perhaps he was just worried about getting home late for dinner.

At the other end of the bar a woman reporter was telling a friend about a recent flight with a bush pilot to an Indian reserve in Northern Canada. It was a rough flight, apparently, because she was describing how she had been airsick and was sure they would crash in the remote forest.

Peters was drinking with another *Gazette* editor, who had accompanied him on this out-of-town trip, and who had recently written a story involving a doctor accused of malpractice. The doctor had threatened to sue the paper for libel if the story was printed. The suit never materialized, but a dispute later arose among the paper's staff over the published story's handling. Peters had been obliged to settle it, and the man who wrote the story was feeling a bit sheepish at having caused so much trouble.

"I suppose you must get tired of straightening out hassles," he said.

Peters, who would soon have to deal with two bona fide lawsuits arising out of other stories, while overseeing the coverage of events as diverse as a police shoot-out with a well-known bank robber and the exposure of a ring smuggling illegal aliens into the country, sipped his drink, looked at the animated, gesturing people around him, and smiled.

"No," he replied. "I don't. I love this crazy business."

The reply was typical not only of Peters, whose personality reveled in trouble and challenges, but of newsmen and women in general. Those who go into journalism—and stay in it—are rarely nine-to-fivers, the kind who punch a time clock in boredom every morning and live only for payday. With few exceptions, they are of another breed.

A good reporter, working on a good story, lives and breathes his work. It becomes a sort of addiction, as strong as but infinitely more rewarding than any narcotic drug. Some police detectives are that way about their jobs, as are many medical doctors and other professionals. Money is important to them. They need it to live. But the real reason they stay in their jobs is because they love doing them.

Working in journalism provides many rewards, some tangible and some intangible, but one of the industry's major sources of satisfaction is its public service aspect. No democracy, from a local city council to the national governments in Washington, D.C., or Ottawa, can function unless its citizens know what is going on around them, understand public issues, and are able to make informed choices when they vote in an election or sign a petition. The media in our society, newspapers, television, and magazines, are probably the largest single source of information available to the public. Without such sources, nobody would know what was happening and democratic government would be impossible.

If the Washington *Post,* Los Angeles *Times,* and other papers had not spent a good deal of time and money delving into the workings of the government of former President Nixon, for example, the American people might never have known that their government was fighting an undeclared, illegal war in Cambodia or that the White House staff was engaging in burglary, sabotage, forgery, and other "dirty tricks" to destroy its political enemies. Because journalists exposed these things, the public was able to react and force the lawbreakers out of office.

If local weekly newspapers did not print stories revealing the workings of local school boards or county boards of supervisors, the public would have no watchdog to let them know whether the roofing contractor putting asphalt on the elementary school roof was using inferior material and slipshod construction methods. The contractor might get away with it, after bribing a board member, and the taxpayers would end up losers.

Performing the watchdog role isn't the only form of public service available to journalists. A news story published in the Muskegon (Mich.) *Chronicle* on Thanksgiving Day, 1967, about a steeplejack who had fallen from a water tower and suffered serious head injuries, resulted in a flood of contributions from readers to help pay his medical bills. The injured man, whose family was in Missouri, was sent back home after a lengthy stay in hospital. The money sent in by readers paid for the trip.

Newspaper stories have also helped locate missing persons, enabling them to be reunited with long-lost family, raised money for the relief of flood and other disaster victims, and created support for public service projects ranging from the building of new hospitals to the financing of scientific research. A newspaper that takes its responsibilities seriously can be a potent force for good, and the reporters who write articles of a public service nature can truly say they are helping make the world a better place in which to live.

Creative Satisfaction

In addition to its public service aspect, journalism also provides those involved in it with considerable creative satisfaction. When the day's edition of the paper rolls off the presses, there is a solid, physical product there. The reporter sees his story in print, the photographer sees his pictures, and the makeup editor sees the overall effect of the design he chose for each page. If they did their jobs well, they can take pride in the final product and, sometimes, hear actual praise from readers who write or phone to say how much they appreciated the effort.

Like a finish carpenter or cabinetmaker, who stands back and looks with satisfaction on the work of his hands, journalists are craftsmen and craftswomen.

This feeling of satisfaction is often evident after deadline, when copies of the paper are distributed in the newsroom. Reporters can frequently be seen sitting at their desks, reading the stories they wrote as they appeared in the paper. They don't have to read them. They already know what they said. But there the words are, in the paper with the reporter's by-line above them, and they look at the stories anyway, just like a carpenter looking at a newly finished chair. They read the stories over and over and feel a secret joy when a letter to the editor comes in praising their work.

More formal, and lucrative, recognition is also available. There are many awards offered annually to reporters, photographers, and broadcasters, ranging from the prestigious Pulitzer Prize to a multitude of lesser-known journalism prizes. Some include cash awards up to several thousand dollars, whereas others involve only a trophy or framed award certificate. All provide a boost to the newsman's ego and increase his standing among his peers. They are pats on the back, and very much appreciated.

Sometimes, especially in the case of columnists or feature writers, collections of particularly good work, of stories that have literary merit, may be published in book form. Yesterday's paper usually ends up in the trash, but books are kept and reread for years, and the reporter who publishes one has the satisfaction of knowing his effort will reach that many more people and have that much greater effect. It is a good feeling.

Educational Experience

A year on general assignment at a daily newspaper is worth several years of formal schooling. It is an education in itself, a cram course in hard knocks and the vagaries of human nature.

Take the port and marine reporter of one large metropolitan daily, for example. He had been on the beat less than a year when he was sent to interview the president of a longshoremen's union local, about whom he had written in a recent column. The union chief did not like the column. He pushed the reporter out of the second-floor window of his office. The reporter landed on the hood of a car, whose driver stepped on the gas and took off with the reporter spread-eagled on the hood, hanging onto the radio antenna for dear life.

The reporter's injuries were limited to cuts and bruises, but he never forgot the lesson learned that day: don't stand near an open window in a longshoremen's union office.

Other lessons young reporters learn are more subtly imparted. They learn that people are sometimes capable of telling lies and weaving plots so deviously complex as to be virtual works of art. These can often make the reporter who fails to see through them look like a fool. Even simple plots can trap the unwary.

For example, a reporter was once approached by a woman with a severely retarded child. The woman, who told the reporter she was on welfare, said she wanted to place her child in a special school but had no money to pay the costs of the classes. The reporter, being good-hearted, wrote a story about the woman's plight, and readers who saw it began sending money to the paper to help her.

Unknown to the reporter, the woman was a crook. She had worked in carnivals and frequently exhibited her child as a freak on the midway. In this case, she had been put up to approaching the paper by a local hoodlum, who saw it as a chance to make more money than the nickels and dimes carnival attractions rake in.

The money sent in by readers was duly turned over to the mother, who split it with the local hood and left town, leaving her daughter behind, abandoned. Needless to say, the paper looked ridiculous to the readers who had sent in money, and the reporter felt terrible. The child was eventually placed with foster parents. Nobody ever heard from the mother again.

Fortunately, for every negative experience like that described, the young reporter will have five or six positive ones. As a general rule, honest, warm-hearted people outnumber crooks. During the 1967 riots in Detroit, for example, more than forty persons were killed and hundreds of rioters set fires and damaged property. But *thousands* of people worked to put the fires out, restore order, and help each other. Reporters for the Detroit *News* and the Detroit *Free Press* who covered the story saw fire fighters risking their lives to save homes, working long hours without rest. They saw neighbors opening their homes to those who had been burned out, providing food and shelter to strangers. Whites and blacks helped each other, as well as hurt each other.

Reporters meet all kinds of people, from sharecroppers to presidents, and learn that human nature in all its variety is an inexhaustible source of interest. The famous and the infamous are only human, and journalists see firsthand evidence of it every day. The reporter who interviewed former U.S. Attorney General John Mitchell (later imprisoned in the wake of the Watergate investigations) at a reception before a 1969 speech, discovered that Mitchell was a hockey fan. He had played hockey in his university days and was able to discuss the Stanley Cup chances of various NHL teams at length and with authority. How many people can say that they have discussed hockey with a public figure whose name will be mentioned in history texts for centuries to come? The same reporter also had the opportunity to hear the founder of the United Auto Workers Union, Walter Reuther, tell the story of the famous "Battle of the Overpass" that marked the union's birth; to interview former President Gerald Ford when he was still a Congressman, and to welcome home the first American citizens to visit Communist China after the cold war.

The things learned in such encounters are more valuable than years of schooling.

Battle Fever

Journalists, particularly those who cover politics or become involved in investigative stories, discover after awhile that they have caught a kind of "battle fever," a thirst to be in the thick of public controversy and a desire to influence the direction of public policy. They realize that those who write the news have a surprising amount of power to change the society around them, its laws and its structures, and that this power can be used for good ends. When the stories they write have effect and policy is changed because of them, they feel as if their work has really counted.

One reporter spent several months investigating a black-market adoption racket in a major city, which involved the selling of babies to childless people. The stories he wrote caused the government to introduce legislation to prevent such abuses, and the government report introducing the proposed new laws mentioned that the news stories had prompted the lawmakers' move.

Such direct evidence that the story had done its job was heartening. Equally pleasing to the reporter, however, was the long game of wits that had preceded publication of the articles. To gain information on the persons handling the adoptions, the reporter had been obliged to pose as someone who wanted to adopt a child and who had money to spend. Another reporter working with him had posed as an unwed mother with a child to sell. When the deception was revealed, one woman involved in the racket was amazed. She was a wily old con-woman, slick and clever, and in a voice shot through with indignation asked the reporter: "You mean *you've* been conning *me?*" It was probably the first time in her life that the tables had been turned on her.

Instead of her swindling other people, she had been taken in by the reporters. Such things whet the investigative reporter's appetite to do more stories in the same vein.

Journalists who cover politics, too, inevitably become fascinated by the debates that fly thick and fast over various political issues. They also get to know the politicians themselves and before long develop fairly well-informed opinions of their own about the laws and the operation of government.

When they write articles or columns about these issues, whether involving the future of nuclear power plants, the size of welfare checks, or any other subject, they cannot avoid taking sides in at least some of the debates. They end up opposing some politicians and supporting others, and the politicians are quick to fight back. The journalists' articles are attacked in speeches in the legislature, in letters to the editor, and in opposing newspapers.

The journalists defend their opinions with gusto and, in fact, end up functioning as unofficial legislators who influence the course of debate on issues before the lawmakers. Every voter with a pet peeve would like to have the opportunity to tell the government about it. To be able not only to express that opinion but have it adopted into law would be an exhilarating experience.

Journalists covering politics have many such opportunities and find them a source of great satisfaction.

Unfortunately, not all journalists have wise or responsible opinions on public issues. Some are little better than crackpots, and others are so deeply biased that their articles become untrustworthy. On most large daily papers, the copy editors who read and correct the reporters' stories watch for bias and edit it out whenever it appears. A real effort is made to be objective. But every now and then, especially if the publisher's biases are the same, a slanted or untruthful article can slip into print.

Entering battle over public issues can be a thrilling experience, but it also requires a sense of fairness and responsibility on the journalist's part. It is not always easy for newsmen and women to remain objective, or to discipline themselves and remain honest with the reading public. But the effort must be made.

Climbing the Ladder

The opportunities for advancement in journalism, to earn promotions and higher salaries, are better than in many other fields. The speed with which a young reporter can climb to an editor's job or one of the better writing positions on a newspaper is sometimes a source of amazement to his friends in other lines of work.

A young person with intelligence, drive, and talent can rise from copyboy to managing editor in ten years. I personally know two men who did just that. It is equivalent to an office boy or girl in a corporation rising to vice-president in ten years. One of these two men did not even have a university degree. He had ability.

There are few businesses, large or small, in which such rapid promotions are attainable. Of the two men who gained such rapid advancement, one did it by moving from paper to paper, the other by staying with his original employer.

Not every journalist, of course, wants to end up in management. Most just want to write, and some actually decline offers of promotion that would involve them so deeply in administrative work that they would have no time to write, no chance to get out "on the street." These people set their sights on the top writing jobs, on the key beats, columnists' jobs, or feature writing positions of a newspaper. Such jobs usually carry higher salaries than those of general assignment reporters.

The trail blazed by a young Montreal woman illustrates how a talented person can move up the ladder. This woman took a job as a receptionist at a large daily, but her real goal was to become a reporter. She spent several weeks answering telephones and greeting visitors to the newsroom, acting as a sort of buffer between the paper's assignment editor and the public. She paid attention to the newsroom routine and realized that the assignment editor was terribly overworked. She offered to help in little ways, following up the odd news tip on her own, getting rid of pests and crackpots who would have monopolized the editor's time, and making suggestions now and then on actual news coverage.

Before long she became so valuable to the editor that she was assigned to be his full-time assistant on the City Desk. She was still making a receptionist's salary, but her responsibilities were actually those of an assistant editor. She told her boss about her ambition to be a reporter, and, on a day when he did not have enough people on hand to cover all the assignments, he sent her out to do an interview. She did it extremely well and was soon filling in regularly as a "spare" reporter.

At the end of a year she was put on general assignment full-time, received a salary raise, and *was* a reporter. While on assignment, she met several television news reporters covering the same stories she was handling for her paper. They told her about an opening at a local television station. She applied, got the job, and is now a full-time news broadcaster in Montreal. Every night at 6 and 11 P.M., the ex-receptionist is on screen, reporting the news to two million viewers. Her salary today is at least four times that of a receptionist.

The really pleasant thing about her story is that her ability alone earned those promotions. She did not indulge in office politics or try to flirt with the boss to get ahead. She just did a very good job and took advantage of whatever chances came her way.

The same cannot be said of everyone in the news business. As in every industry, there are a certain number of schemers and plotters who believe the best way to rise is on the bodies of those below them. They try to take credit for other people's work, to make rivals for an important job look bad, and to push themselves forward at every opportunity. Some of these people succeed in gaining high positions and keeping them for awhile. They also succeed in making a lot of enemies and stunting their own personalities.

Eventually some other schemer turns the tables on them, or, if they are actually not very talented, their inability to do the job becomes apparent. They are never truly secure in their jobs or in their personal relations with other employees. Frequently, they are downright miserable people, unhappy with their consciences as well as their work.

Overall, however, advancement in journalism can come very quickly for those who deserve it.

Salaries and Benefits

Back in the 1930's and 1940's journalists were among the lowest-paid people in the work force. They worked long hours, with no compensation for overtime, and took home a pittance. Naturally, the quality of the people who took such ill-paid jobs sometimes left much to be desired. Many had little education, some were alcoholics, and others were so chronically strapped for funds that they took money on the side to do "fluff" stories, articles that were little more than free advertising for a business or a political candidate.

As the reading public became better educated and more sophisticated in their understanding of the issues, however, newspapers realized that their coverage of events had to be well informed and their staffs respectable enough to be taken seriously. They began looking for people with university degrees or expertise in certain subjects. It wasn't long before they discovered that such people would not work for starvation wages.

The North American Newspaper Guild and the International Typographical Union (ITU) were also beginning to organize many big-city dailies and to bargain for higher pay. Salaries began to rise.

Today the salaries paid to reporters and editors at most daily newspapers are competitive with those of equivalent personnel in other local industries. A reporter with five years' experience working for a Chicago daily, for example, earns about the same salary as a five-year man in middle management working for a local manufacturer or in Civil Service.

The recurring cycles of inflation and depression in the economy, of course, make it difficult to predict what salary a reporter in a given city will be making five years from now. In 1970 a yearly salary of $12,000 would go a long way in Cleveland or Detroit. In 1980 the Guild would consider such a figure ridiculous. Differences between regional economies also make it impossible to put precise figures on reporters' pay. In the South, for example, wages in all industries tend to be considerably lower than in the industrialized northern states. A schoolteacher in Detroit in 1979 might make up to $18,000 or $20,000 while the same job in Florida or Georgia might pay $8,000. The same regional differences are found in the newspaper industry.

The rule of thumb, however, is to compare newsmen's pay with that of *local* people holding jobs of roughly equal responsibility. In most cases, the salaries are comparable. There are very few rich reporters, but there are also very few who starve.

Large dailies, the wire services, and dailies that are owned by corporate chains also provide standard fringe benefit packages, including health and life insurance, pension plans, and in some cases profit-sharing programs. Generally, these packages are equivalent to those offered by other local businesses. Sometimes they are better.

Papers whose employees belong to a union often set the standard for other news organizations in their area. To keep the union out, one paper may match or even exceed the salaries paid to reporters at a union paper. The purpose is to keep the staff happy enough so that they won't want to organize. In many cases the plan works, and nonunion people are quite happy with it. In a sense, the nonunion people are getting a free ride, benefiting from the union militancy of their fellow journalists without having to take any risks or go on strike. The end result, however it is reached, is to keep the pay raises coming.

Those who work for weekly newspapers or small magazines aren't always so lucky. Often the paper's revenues are simply too small to permit the owner to pay decent salaries. Sometimes the owner is a skinflint and won't pay acceptable salaries. Since many weeklies only have a two- or three-member editorial staff, it is difficult to organize a union. One weekly had a staff of two, the publisher and one reporter. The reporter tried to get himself recognized as his own legal bargaining unit—as a one-man union local—but failed. The publisher fired him. As young reporters starting out in the business almost always outnumber the available jobs, he was easily replaced.

Generally, the highest salaries in the news industry are paid to television broadcasters. Some, like Barbara Walters or Walter Cronkite, are celebrities, so well known and trusted by the viewing public that they can command salaries equivalent to those of Hollywood stars and sports heroes. Local news commentators, of course, are not in the same league, but their salaries are usually higher than those of their confreres in the print media. Print reporters, naturally, resent this.

They refer disparagingly to the television people as "movie stars" or simply "faces," hired to look pretty and sound pleasant while reading reports written by other people on the station's research staff. It is a clear case of envy and does television news people a disservice.

Radio broadcasters generally make lower salaries than television newsmen, but except at smaller stations that cannot afford to be competitive, radio station owners usually pay salaries roughly equal to those of print journalists.

Syndicates and Free-lancing

Syndicates, organizations that distribute news stories, columns, and feature articles to many newspapers or to a newspaper group, offer another opportunity to journalists. A columnist whose work for a daily newspaper becomes popular may be given the opportunity to sell his column to other papers belonging to the same chain. In some cases, he may swing a deal in which he is allowed to sell the column to nonmember papers, keeping part of the sale proceeds for himself.

Large syndicates, like King Features Syndicate, provide huge markets for journalists and cartoonists, whose work for the syndicate may appear in hundreds of papers. Sometimes payment for such work is in the form of a flat fee per article, sometimes per word, and sometimes on a percentage-of-sales basis. Contracts vary, but the opportunity is there.

One Michigan journalist "syndicated" himself. He wrote several months' worth of weekly columns, mostly humorous ones, and made the rounds of weekly papers. Two or three bought the column, paying him a small fee for it, and he promptly used them in his sales talks to other papers. Eventually he managed to sell the column to a few daily papers and earned enough to support himself full time. He incorporated himself and at last report was making a very good living.

He began as a free lancer, one who does not work full time for any one company but sells his work to whatever paper or magazine is willing to buy it. Free lancers are a hardy breed, but an admirable one. Their working lives and incomes are full of ups and downs.

A free lancer may sell a long, well-researched article to a magazine for $500 to $1,000, pat himself on the back, and then not sell another article for six months. He may work hard on a story he hoped to get $200 for and end up with $50. He can't get mad and quit because he isn't on anyone's full-time staff. It is a rough life. Some of the best journalists in North America, however, are free lancers, and the finest of them, after years of hard apprenticeship, sometimes make very good incomes. Some, like Tom Wolfe in the U.S. or Pierre Berton in Canada, become superstars in the field. They are, however, exceptions.

Although many journalists are highly paid, and even those who are not usually earn enough to provide at least an adequate living, salary should not be the prime motive in choosing a journalism career. One whose main goal in life is to get rich would be better off in some other line of work.

Journalism, like teaching or nursing, is essentially a service profession. Those who follow it have a right to expect to make a decent living, and usually fight to do so, but in the end money is not their object. Like the city editor quoted at the beginning of this chapter, they are in the business because they love it, take pride in it, and would be bored stiff doing anything else.

Sometimes, as the following chapter shows, they wonder whether their commitment to such a career is the kind of commitment that would be made by a sane, well-balanced person. But they make it, nevertheless.

CHAPTER III

Why Newspeople Go Gray

The full moon brings them out:

"Is this the Detroit *Free Press?*" a woman's voice asks over the phone.

"No, this is the Detroit *News,*" replies the copy editor, one eye on the fleeting hands of the clock approaching deadline, the other on the flickering screen of the video computer terminal displaying the story he is editing.

"How can you print things like that about the mayor, and on the front page?" demands the indignant voice.

"Things like what?"

"That atrocious picture on the front page!"

"We don't have a picture of the mayor on page one today, lady . . ."

"Yes, you do! It's a disgusting photograph and . . ."

"That's in the *Free Press,* lady; this is the *News* you've called."

"Yes, I know, but what I want to know is how you can print things like this when you know the mayor . . ."

"The *Free Press* printed it, lady, not us. Call them."

"I want to know why you hate the mayor!"

If the *News* editor is lucky, the irate caller will eventually realize she has telephoned the wrong newspaper and hang up, letting him get back to work. More likely, the caller won't realize her mistake, or want to realize it, and he will be forced to hang up on her. The next day the *News'* managing editor will get a formal complaint from the woman about his rude copy editors. Such scenarios are among the countless minor irritations that are part of every newsman's or newswoman's day.

Often callers want editors to settle bets, assuming that somehow, because they work at a newspaper, their minds must be crammed with trivia: "Say, uh, my buddy and I have this bet whether Six Fingers Orkowicz was the first third baseman in the American League to be spiked by Ty Cobb. Was he?" Other callers are drunk or outright abusive, screaming, swearing at, or threatening the hapless journalist who has the ill fortune to answer the phone when it rings.

Still other calls bring unexpected drama. An Associated Press rewrite man, working the overnight shift in Detroit, once received a long-dis-

A typical newsroom of a daily newspaper as the staff prepares the day's edition (photo by Thomas Pawlick).

tance call from a man in Milwaukee asking for information about a Michigan air crash. The man's wife was on the downed aircraft, and sources in Milwaukee were unable to tell him whether she had survived or died. He called the AP because a Milwaukee newspaper editor had told him the wire service would get bulletins on the crash before the other media. As it turned out, the woman had survived, and the AP man was able to call the husband back and tell him so before official notification had been made. The man was overcome with relief.

In that case the AP journalist did not mind being interrupted by the phone because it had enabled him to perform a humanitarian service.

It is a rare interruption, however, that does not annoy the reporter or editor working on deadline.

Deadlines, as already noted, are sacrosanct in the news business, and newsmen and women are under tremendous pressure to meet them. By the time most journalists have completed their first year or so of apprenticeship, they have become used to writing against the clock and accepted the limitations it imposes as inevitable. Few people, however, can adjust totally to the pressure. Even if only on a subconscious level, it is bound to exact a toll.

The pressure to produce, and its effect on those who feel it, is perhaps most noticeable in the wire services, such as the AP, UPI, or Canadian Press, where the deadline is literally every minute. The work load in a wire service bureau can be so heavy and the competition so hot that the bureau staff are in constant motion, juggling phones and typing until their fingers go stiff throughout their entire shift. As one UPI desk man once joked, grasping his wrist, an expression of horror on his face: "Good grief, my pulse rate's the same as the damn teleprinters!"

Out of eight writers at one wire service bureau in 1970, two had serious alcohol problems, one, a woman, was semi-addicted to tranquilizers, and a fourth was an angry, embittered person forever picking fights. The pressure at work, of course, was not solely responsible for their problems, but it certainly aggravated any existing psychological difficulties. As the pioneering research of Dr. Hans Selye has amply demonstrated, stress can have marked effects on both the human mind and body, causing physical and mental deterioration. The kind of deadline pressure generated in a wire service bureau can easily produce an overdose of stress. So can the pressure on the copydesk at a daily paper or at an understaffed weekly.

The assignment editor at one Montreal paper provided a classic example of the effects of stress. Before being promoted to the assignment editor's post he had been a quiet, easygoing person with a subtle sense of humor. After six months as assignment editor, a post noted for its high pressure, he had become an obnoxious grouch, never smiling, lashing out in sudden anger at anyone who irritated him. He eventually was reshuffled to another post, whereupon he became his old, pleasant self again. Other journalists have been less fortunate. Some develop stomach ulcers, others develop emotional problems so serious as to disrupt their family life or lead to divorce.

Not all personalities react to the stresses of the news business in such negative ways, of course. Some people react very little, and others seem to thrive under a certain amount of pressure. The same can be said of those in other high-stress professions, from police work to air traffic control. The response to pressure varies with every individual, affecting some more than others.

Whatever its effect, stress is a factor to be considered by anyone interested in a journalism career—and deadline pressure is not its only cause.

Conflict and Controversy

Journalists, by the very nature of their work, inevitably become involved in conflict, controversy, and confrontation. In reporting on disputes between others, they become caught up in those disputes, often against their will. For example, reporters and photographers covering protest demonstrations or picket marches routinely run the risk of being injured or arrested if the demonstration becomes violent. A line of truncheon-swinging police wading into a shouting mob is unlikely to distinguish between demonstrators and newsmen. Many reporters have been beaten by police, or even by the demonstrators, and photographers have had expensive camera equipment smashed in sidewalk scuffles.

The Montreal reporter mentioned in Chapter I who saw the union picketer to whom he was speaking cut down by a shotgun blast could easily have been cut down himself. Newsmen covering the antiwar demonstrations in Chicago during the Democratic Party's 1968 National Presidential Convention were teargassed and beaten along with the protesters.

Reporters and photographers covering fires, floods, and other natural disasters also run the risk of personal injury, as do those covering robberies in progress, hostage-taking incidents, or other situations in which police and lawbreakers may shoot it out. A stray bullet could as easily hit a reporter at the scene as a police officer.

Sometimes the bullets coming at a reporter are not strays, but are deliberately intended to hit the journalist. Such was the case with Canadian investigative reporter Ralph Noseworthy, who narrowly escaped death in 1975 when a would-be assassin fired a pistol at him through the window of his car. Noseworthy was driving home along a lonely stretch of highway in Quebec when a car behind him flashed its headlights to high beam and pulled out to pass him. Noseworthy instinctively lifted his foot from the accelerator pedal to slow his car and allow the other vehicle to pass more easily. This gesture of courtesy saved his life. As the other automobile swerved around him, a gun was fired and the bullet passed a fraction of an inch in front of the reporter's face. If he had not slowed down, it would have struck him squarely in the temple.

Other reporters have been less fortunate. Arizona newsman Don Bolles, investigating political corruption in his state in the early 1970's, was fatally wounded when a bomb planted in his car by a hired killer exploded. Those responsible for his murder were later arrested and convicted, and the series of articles he had begun writing was carried on by others. A "task force" of reporters from other papers around the country, all specialists in investigative work, descended on Arizona after the murder and together conducted a massive scrutiny of the state and local governments. The resulting stories were printed in newspapers across the United States. They could not, of course, bring Bolles back to life.

Not all reporters who cover organized crime or who specialize in uncovering political or other forms of corruption run such deadly risks. Actual killings or attempts on the lives of journalists are rare. Generally, those involved in organized crime prefer to attack witnesses who might give information to reporters rather than to attack the reporters themselves. They know that physical assault against a newsman may result in more publicity, rather than less, and consequently stop short of violence.

Frequently, however, they attempt to frighten or bluff an overinquisitive reporter by means of threats designed to make him believe he is in danger. A reporter working on a sensitive story may begin receiving anonymous telephone calls at 3 A.M. in which "heavy breathers" warn him of the dire consequences of publishing what he knows. Sometimes reporters are followed by men in suspicious-looking cars. Usually this kind of intimidation ceases once the article in question is published, those who stood to lose by seeing it in print having concluded that after the horse has escaped there is no point closing the stable door. Experienced reporters know this, and generally they do not take the anonymous threats seriously. Nevertheless, such harassment can get on a person's nerves and be disturbing for a reporter's family.

Physical danger is also part and parcel of the working lives of correspondents and photographers assigned to cover warfare. The newsmen and women who accompany fighting troops often come home, like the soldiers they write about, in a pine box. One such casualty was Ernie Pyle, one of the greatest of American war correspondents, who was shot and killed by a Japanese soldier in the Pacific theater during World War II.

Other correspondents have lost their lives in Korea, Vietnam, Latin America, and Africa, victims of guns, bombs, or bayonets.

Libel and Other Dangers

Although only a small minority of journalists must face physical danger in their work, virtually every reporter and editor must live with the ever-present threat of a libel suit being brought against them. Some must also face threats to their personal job security, particularly on smaller papers where advertisers wield more influence than on larger dailies.

Laws against slander and libel exist to protect the good name and reputation of innocent persons who can suffer injury if untrue or malicious things are said or written about them. Such laws, obviously, are needed in any society but especially in our own, where rumors, lies, or insults can reach an audience of thousands, perhaps millions, of people through a single television broadcast or one edition of a major newspaper.

Libel is defined in the *Oxford Dictionary* as a "published, false statement damaging to a person's reputation." Slander is defined as "spoken defamation." Unfortunately for journalists, innocent persons are not the only ones protected by laws against slander and libel. All too often the guilty find ways to take shelter under the legal jargon of the statute books and use the law to thwart or punish those who try to expose them.

For example, a major national magazine once published a story about a Mafia Don, describing the rackets in which he was involved and his relations with other criminals. Much of the material in the story, though true, came from anonymous sources whose identities could not be revealed.

The crime boss, who was wealthy enough to hire a virtual army of lawyers, sued the magazine for libel and, after a long-drawn-out trial, won his case. Luckily for the magazine, the judge, knowing exactly what the situation was, awarded only symbolic damages of one dollar to the Don. The underworld chieftain's aim in bringing the suit—namely, to frighten other publications away from covering mob activities—was thus foiled.

Other publications have not been so lucky. One reporter, covering a series of government hearings on organized crime, listened as a witness—who happened to be a police officer—testified before the crime commission about the activities of a local mob associate. The witness, testifying before a formal government commission, was immune from being prosecuted for libel; however, according to the technicalities of law in this particular instance, the reporter was not immune. He wrote a story for his paper quoting the witness, whose charges had not been proven, and the mob associate promptly sued the paper. He won. The paper was found guilty and had to pay a known criminal $50,000 in damages.

In this case the paper paid the damages, not the reporter. In another case a "hanging judge" in Windsor, Ontario, found a paper guilty of libel and in his judgment ordered that the reporter himself pay the damages out of his own pocket. The sum was considerable, and it was specified that the reporter's paper could not in any way compensate him for the loss.

In many cases criminals and other not-so-innocent parties bring libel suits even though they know they can't win them. They sue as a form of harassment, hoping to tie up the reporter and his paper's lawyers in court, costing them money in legal fees, for as long as possible. Sometimes they file suit simply to make themselves look good, to make the public believe they are innocent.

Any reporter who must defend his personal honesty and professional reputation in a court of law is in for a grueling experience. If the editors of his paper lack integrity and fail to support him, he may face the test alone.

Still other journalists find themselves in court not because the truth of what they've written has been challenged, but because what they wrote was all *too* true. Reporters may be called before official bodies, from a grand jury to a federal court, to provide testimony against a lawbreaker. If the information the reporter obtained came from persons who asked him to keep their names secret, the reporter may be caught in a terrible dilemma. A court, ruling that his informants' names are needed to bolster the case against a defendant, may order the reporter to break his promise and reveal the names. Several reporters who refused to do so have been convicted of contempt of court and forced to serve prison sentences.

The prospect of such legal complications makes experienced newsmen cautious. Stories of a controversial nature are gone over by the newspaper's own lawyers before publication, read, reread, and rewritten to avoid libel. But no matter how hard a publication may try, it can never be sure of immunity. One celebrated case is a prime example. A news photographer took a picture of a man and woman holding hands in a local park on Valentine's Day, and the picture ran on page one. The photographer had naively neglected to ask the couple's permission before taking his shot. He lived to regret it. The man was married—not to his partner in the park—and his wife saw the picture. A divorce proceeding was launched, and the husband sued the paper. He won.

Censorship Versus Conscience

The physical and legal dangers discussed so far do not exhaust the list of problems journalists must face. Of equal importance, and likely to produce just as much stress, are the moral crises brought about by that bane of all writers: censorship.

Censorship, the suppression of or refusal to publish all or part of the news, has been an obstacle for American journalists since the beginning—as the closure of Benjamin Harris' colonial-era newspaper illustrated.

Politicians and other influential people on this continent have been no more willing to permit scrutiny of their affairs by a free press than their counterparts around the world. Fortunately, however, the governments of the United States and Canada are democracies, and the tradition of a free press is strong in both countries. Although private attacks on individual journalists may sometimes take place (in frontier days, tarring and feathering of editors was a popular pastime), official government efforts to control or muzzle the press have been minimal compared to those of other nations.

Even in wartime, when censorship of military news by the governments of other countries is almost always very strict, North American journalists have been remarkably free to report developments without hindrance. For example, during World War II, although the fall of Bataan Island and the battering of American troops on the beach at Anzio, Italy, shook morale at home, both events were reported in the U.S. and Canadian press. During the Vietnam War, the shameful massacre of innocent civilians by U.S. troops at My Lai was also widely reported in the American press, despite the U.S. government's obvious interest in keeping such embarrassing incidents secret.

Such freedom would never be permitted to journalists working for, say, the Soviet news agency Tass, or for newspapers in other countries with authoritarian governments.

The fact that North American journalists enjoy more freedom than their counterparts in other countries does not, however, mean that they are immune from attempts to suppress what they report. During the Vietnam War and the subsequent Watergate investigations, the administration of then-President Nixon made a concerted effort to stir up public support for press censorship. Spearheaded by Vice-President Spiro T. Agnew, a propaganda campaign against the "effete snobs" of the press was pushed with great vigor. The campaign failed when Agnew was subsequently charged with income tax evasion and forced to resign from office in disgrace—followed not long afterward by Nixon himself— but the chilling effect on newsmen was a long time wearing off.

Perhaps even more dangerous—and harder for the individual newsman or woman to fight—are the insidious internal attacks upon the truth made by biased or fearful journalists themselves. Overt government attacks on press freedom are obvious and create their own opposition. Self-censorship by the editors of a newspaper or bias on the part of its reporters are more difficult to detect and sometimes impossible to prevent.

Reporters for a major wire service witnessed an example of this kind of self-censorship during the Vietnam War, an incident that backfired on those responsible for it. A Pulitzer Prize-winning war correspondent in the field had sent back a dispatch describing an incident in which U.S. troops had looted and burned a town in the war zone— an act contrary to the rules of warfare. The correspondent's editors in New York, who supported the war, were upset by the story.

A decision was made to suppress the story, and it was duly removed from the wires leading to the newsrooms of the nation's daily newspapers. Unfortunately for the censors, however, there are *two* copies of stories, one for newspapers, the other for television and radio news. The copy intended for newspapers was destroyed, but that for broadcast stations was overlooked. The result was that television stations and radio newsmen all over the country were reporting the story while the newspapers knew nothing about it.

Irate newspaper editors, angry at being scooped by their electronic competitors, complained loudly to the wire service's directors, and the news agency was acutely embarrassed. It took them a long time to reestablish their credibility.

Similar events are common at the local level, especially when controversial subjects are in question that stir the emotions of the public and journalists alike. The battles for black civil rights, women's liberation, and unionization of farm workers, the controversies over pornography, abortion, and homosexual rights, have all prompted varying degrees of self-censorship and biased reporting in the press. In the 1930's, the same kinds of bias could be seen in newspaper coverage of strikes and the development of labor unions. It was as rare to find a newspaper story opposing legalized abortion in 1970 as it was to find one supporting the United Auto Workers Union in 1930. In some cases, the bias of the press is "on the right side"; in others, it is not. But whatever side a newspaper supports, doing so through slanted news coverage is reprehensible.

Writing Responsibly

Frequently an honest reporter trying to write the news responsibly can be put in a bad position by his editors or publisher. Sometimes, the conflicts that arise are downright agonizing.

Such was the case in 1977 when a reporter on a major metropolitan daily was told by his city editor to "go out and do a sob story" on a local family whose father was being held prisoner in Uganda, then ruled by the erratic, brutal dictator, Idi Amin. The imprisoned man's daughter-in-law worked at the newspaper as a receptionist, and it was she who first tipped the editors to the story.

"We held a family conference and decided to go to the paper for help," a family member told the reporter. "We were reluctant to do it, because the wrong kind of story might put him in even more danger. But everything else has failed." Amin's secret police had murdered thousands of political prisoners, and the mercurial Amin, whom some observers believed to be insane, was known to order executions of prisoners on the whim of the moment. He eagerly sought publicity that made him look powerful and important but was likely to fly into a sudden rage—and order an execution—at a critical article or broadcast. Obviously, it would be a tall order to write an article that would tell the story accurately and bring pressure on Amin to release his captive, but that would not be so negative as to make the dictator fly into a rage. At first, after talking to the family and consulting with government diplomats, the reporter decided it was best not to publish a story at all. Everyone agreed that a simple inquiry from the paper, directed to Ugandan diplomats in North America and hinting broadly that adverse publicity might follow harm done to the prisoner, would be sufficient at the start. If the inquiry brought no results, then a mildly worded article, noting that the prisoner's family was seeking information on his case, would be tried. Any direct criticism of Amin was to be avoided, at least for the time being.

The reporter thought his editors would agree to this policy, assuming that since a man's life was at stake—a man whose relative was an employee of the paper—they would be willing to tread lightly. He was wrong.

"What do you mean wait?" demanded his irritated city editor. "This is a great sob story. We should run it now, before anybody else gets it." It was pointed out to the reporter that the paper had only recently published a syndicated story by another newsman telling of his own frightening experience as a prisoner in Uganda, that the paper had paid money for the right to reprint it, and now that the editors had a chance to get "a Uganda story of our own" they didn't want to lose it. The fact that the price of publishing their "own" Uganda story might be the death of an innocent man seemed not to be a factor in the editors' calculations.

The reporter was shocked by such callousness but had an ace up his sleeve. The family had not yet talked to any other newspaper, naively believing that being loyal to the paper where the daughter-in-law worked was in their best interest. He phoned the family, explained the situation, and obtained their promise that they would not give an interview to anyone except him, personally. He then went back to his editors and told them that he would not write the story yet and that the family would not talk to any other reporter. He was risking his job to do this, as it was tantamount to refusing an assignment. The editors, however, knew that they couldn't do anything about it except fire the reporter. They agreed to wait and not publish an immediate story.

That agreement marked the start of a months-long battle between the reporter and his editors over the handling of the story, a battle that eventually contributed to the reporter's decision to resign.

When the first of several articles on the imprisoned man was finally scheduled to appear, the paper's editors wanted to sensationalize it, putting in gory descriptions of how Amin's other prisoners had been murdered, describing the "bloodstained, cockroach-infested" jail where prisoners were held, and referring to Amin himself as a "butcher." The descriptions of both the jail and Amin were accurate, but putting them in the story at that point might well have angered Uganda's government and gotten the prisoner killed.

Only after the reporter had argued for nearly half an hour, at some points shouting, did the editors agree to tone down the story. Despite their agreement, the reporter discovered subsequently that the inflammatory statements had *not* been taken out of the article. He had to take them out himself, in the composing room, asking a printer to remove them from the page before the final printing plates were made.

As it turned out, the battle could have been avoided. The imprisoned man was eventually discovered to have been machine-gunned during an abortive escape attempt even before the newspaper became involved in the case. For several months the reporter and the prisoner's family had been working to free a man who was already dead.

The fact that the editors, in this case the city editor and managing editor, of a major daily paper were willing to ignore the welfare of an innocent person, risking his life for the sake of sensationalism, was nevertheless profoundly shocking to the reporter. The fact that a relative of one of the paper's own employees was being put in danger was even more shocking.

The reporter resigned from the paper that same year, and when his story announcing the Uganda prisoner's death finally appeared it was in another newspaper. The experience of having been responsible for the life of another human being, and having to fight for months to prevent his own employers from recklessly getting that human being killed, was a heavy emotional strain.

Not every news person will b nvolved in such life-or-death dramas, but most will have conflicts of conscience of some kind and will be forced more than once to choose between what an editor wants and what they know to be the responsible thing to do.

The choice is not always easy. The sensation-seeking editors in the Uganda prisoner case were, after all, only exhibiting an extreme version of a kind of mental outlook common among journalists. Even the reporter in this instance had been guilty of less-pronounced, but similar, aberrations in the past. The fact is that journalists, after covering many bizarre and often violent events, gradually become anesthetized. They start to look on human suffering not as suffering, but as a source of reader interest, as news rather than pain.

A reporter on the Detroit *News* once inadvertently provided an example. He was reading another writer's article about a local murder case and had come to the part describing the more violent aspects of the crime. He looked up from the page, an expression of admiration on his face, and exclaimed: "Wow! What a *great* murder!"

Reporters must sometimes make a conscious effort to avoid becoming cynical or callous, to avoid looking on the misfortunes of others as so many "great murders."

There are, of course, many other drawbacks inherent in a journalism career, some major and some minor in nature. News people, for example, almost always "know more than they can print," and the burden of that knowledge can be weighty after awhile. The city hall reporter may know which aldermen are crooks but be unable to say so in print for lack of proof. He or she may know of a crooked cop taking payoffs but be forced to remain silent to avoid libel dangers.

Overall, however, the strains of the profession are not so great that they cannot be endured and overcome. The rewards of being a journalist, most of the time, outweigh the penalties. In the opinion of those who have a true vocation for this way of life, the rewards *far* outweigh the drawbacks.

Like the editor quoted earlier, they "love this crazy business," warts and all.

CHAPTER IV

What Managing Editors Want

The hiring at most newspapers is done by the managing editor, although sometimes the city editor is also accorded this privilege.

What a managing editor looks for in a potential employee is a person, male or female, who can speak well, who looks presentable, who seems aware of what's happening in the world of public affairs, and who can write a clear declarative sentence without botching either the spelling or the grammar.

Managing editors also like to hire people who are scramblers, who are aggressive and willing to work hard for a story.

They tend to shy away from slobs who smell like year-old sweat socks, people who slouch in their chairs during an interview, people who seem shy or who mumble when they speak, and people who can't prove that they can write clearly and type at least 40 words per minute on a typewriter.

There was a period in the late 1950's and early 1960's when a university degree was also considered a necessary qualification for a newspaper job. A degree in journalism was preferred. The disappointing performance of many degree-holders on the job, however, has led to a partial relaxation of this requirement. Having a university degree still helps, but a high school graduate who has educated him or herself can still break into journalism. A year or two of junior college can provide a real advantage.

Editors, in short, are more interested in what you know than where you learned it.

The Reasons Why

Why should a newspaper editor care whether his reporters can speak well and converse easily? Broadcast journalists who must deliver their reports orally on television or radio have an obvious reason to be good speakers, but journalists in the print media *write* their stories. Why should speaking ability be important for them?

The answer is that reporters get the majority of the information they put in a news story from other people, from those they interview, and at least half of the skill needed to conduct an interview is verbal.

The ability to express his own thoughts aloud clearly, precisely, and using a wide vocabulary is crucial for a journalist. It makes it possible for the person being interviewed to understand the reporter's questions, thus avoiding confusion and ambiguity. Sometimes a reporter's speaking ability also helps those being interviewed to express themselves better. A well-chosen word or phrase spoken by the journalist may help an interview subject to crystallize and explain his own ideas, expanding on what the reporter said and giving "good quotes."

A good reporter doesn't just walk up to a person who might have the information he is seeking and start blurting out questions, with no preliminary planning or personal introduction. In many cases, he could end up with a black eye for his efforts, or at least frighten an interview subject into silence. The experienced journalist tries, as far as circumstances will allow, to plan his questions in advance and to make his initial approach to an interview subject in a way designed to reassure the person and put him or her in a friendly mood.

This isn't always possible, of course, especially in crowded settings such as at an airport press conference. An interview subject who is already hostile to newsmen—for example, a politician who has been severely criticized by the reporter's paper—may also be impossible to put in a good mood. Nevertheless, an effort is generally made to gain the subject's confidence, and the questions to be asked are thought out beforehand.

The reporter must be a fairly good judge of character and mood, able to "read" his interview subject the way a good public speaker sizes up his audience. He should be able to sense when the person being questioned is becoming angry, frightened, or relaxed and be able to adjust his own manner and tone of voice to his subject's mood. The ability to blend in with a group and adopt, at least for the moment, the group's outlook and mannerisms can also be useful.

For example, a newspaper in a northern apple-growing region had been trying without success to get a group of Jamaican migrant workers who had come north to harvest apples to talk about wages and working conditions in the orchards. The paper's efforts were futile until one of its reporters, a fourth-year journalism student working at the paper part time, happened to mention that he had lived in Jamaica for several years and spoke the colorful Jamaican dialect fluently. He was sent on the story and immediately established a friendly rapport with the field workers. They trusted him because he spoke their own dialect and could recall things "at home" that other people in the northern region knew nothing about.

It should be evident that an excessively shy person, or one who cannot socialize or talk easily with strangers, will have a tough time as a reporter. Meeting and gaining the confidence of complete strangers is part of a reporter's everyday life, and a shy journalist will either get over his shyness quickly or lose his job equally fast.

It should also be obvious that a reporter ought to look presentable and keep a reasonably neat appearance. A filthy slob trailing dust is a lot less likely to gain a stranger's confidence or induce people to talk freely than someone who looks neat and efficient.

Being aware of current affairs is another basic prerequisite in a potential journalist. Ignorance may be bliss, but praising the military acumen of Israeli General Moshe Dayan at a banquet, say, for the ambassador of Libya could get a well-meaning young news person in trouble. Anyone seriously aspiring to become a journalist should be aware of the world around him, of its political and social history and problems and the relationships of its various peoples to each other. The more a reporter knows about the world in general, the better he will be able to interpret and explain the small corner of it that is his beat.

For example, a labor reporter covering a strike by local dockworkers in a port city might, if he were unaware of affairs elsewhere, file a story stating only that the strike had begun, how much the strikers wanted in wages, and how much management was willing to pay them. A reporter who followed events in the rest of the world, however, might be able to report that one of the ships not being loaded during the dock strike was supposed to be carrying wheat to a distant nation in the grip of famine, where thousands might die if the promised wheat failed to arrive.

The difference between reporting all of the news or part of it often lies in the journalist's awareness of events outside his own special area.

Writing Ability

A myth that ought to be destroyed is the idea that to be a reporter you must have marked writing talent, that only those with the literary originality of a Hemingway can write the news. Certainly, editors are interested in applicants who show a flair for writing and have a colorful style. But that isn't the only type of applicant they're interested in.

The colorful stylist may become a feature writer or columnist, but to cover a regular news beat and write a clear, readable account of what you see doesn't take literary genius. It only takes organization and hard work. A reporter may not have a prayer of winning the Nobel Prize in literature, but if he can write down clearly and concisely what the local alderman said at a meeting, that's all it takes.

Unfortunately, too few candidates for reporting jobs seem to have taken the trouble to learn the basics of English grammar. Some write so poorly it is difficult to believe they are even employing the English language. Particularly doubtful are those who have taken the scrambled jargon of the sociologist or government bureaucrat as a model, the sort who would render an ordinary sentence such as "Jack smacked Mack" as "John interfaced violently with Matthew."

A solid grasp of how nouns, verbs, adjectives, and adverbs work together to create sentences and express what people see and feel is absolutely essential in newspaper work. Grammar is not so difficult to comprehend that only a genius should make the attempt. Really, it is no more difficult than learning to add and subtract. A person who will not make the effort to master the subject has no business in newspaper work.

The medical writer at one large metropolitan daily had never mastered it. How she got her job in the first place, no one on the copydesk knew, but the stories she filed were the worst mishmash of confused, disconnected, grammatically meaningless phrases imaginable. The city editor gave out her stories to edit as punishment for people on the copydesk who had fouled up on something else. Her stories were also used to initiate editors who had just joined the paper. These unfortunates would be given one of the medical writer's stories to edit their first day on the job, and the look of dismay on their faces as they read the copy was a source of endless merriment to their sadistic colleagues.

When the medical writer quit to take another job, the copydesk staff cheered. That woman, who away from the typewriter was a very nice person, should never have gone into journalism. Hopefully, she will not return to it.

Personality Traits

A good reporter should be able to overcome any inherent shyness and socialize easily with people. Managing editors look for evidence of this ability when they interview prospective employees. But sociability isn't the only personality trait sought in a journalist. A reporter must be tenacious and stubborn, as well as aggressive when the occasion warrants it. He or she must also be resourceful and even somewhat crafty.

Useful too are such attributes as a healthy curiosity, the ability to keep a cool head under pressure, a sense of fairness and objectivity, and—last but not least—a well-developed set of personal ethics.

The people a reporter meets while gathering information for a news story are frequently uncooperative, if not downright hostile. Getting information out of them can be like pulling teeth. At the scene of a five-alarm fire, for example, a fire department lieutenant may be too busy to talk to a reporter. Worried about the safety of his men, the functioning of his equipment, and the progress of the flames, he may find the interruption of some nosy newsman's questions intolerable. More than one polite young cub reporter has asked a fire fighter, "How did the fire start, lieutenant?" only to be told, "Get the hell out of my way, you jerk!"

A reporter must be persistent and have a thick skin. He or she must be able to keep after that fire lieutenant until he answers the question or be able to find someone else who will. Being naturally stubborn is a great help in such situations. So is being resourceful.

One cub reporter, covering his first big fire, was rebuffed by several fire officials at the scene until, glancing up at the roof of the burning building, he noticed a fireman waving his arms at the crowd below. It turned out that a hose was wanted up on the roof, and there were no firemen free to lug it up there. The fire fighter was calling for help from the crowd. The reporter saw his chance. He picked up the heavy coil of hose and, aided by another bystander, lugged it up a fire escape to the roof. The grateful fireman told his lieutenant about it later, and the reporter was given an exclusive, in-depth interview. Not only did he have all of his questions answered, but his own experience lugging the hose onto the hot roof, smoke billowing around him and flames crackling, provided terrific color for his story. The article made page one, with a by-line.

Tenacity can pay dividends in many situations.

Another reporter, rebuffed with a curt "No comment" when he tried to get a politician to respond during a press conference to charges that his government had discovered evidence of corruption among cabinet members, refused to give up. He telephoned the politician later at his office and was again told, "No comment." Finally, he telephoned the politician at home in the evening. This time the politician finally quit resisting. He admitted that a cabinet member was guilty of taking bribes, named the man, and said he had been ordered to resign. The reporter had a page one story. If he had given up after one or two "No comments," he would have had nothing.

A journalist must be aggressive enough to ask hard or awkward questions, questions that may anger or annoy the person being interviewed but that must be answered if the truth is to come out. He cannot afford to be timid. Former President Nixon, forced to resign in the wake of the Watergate scandals of the 1970's, once assured the American people: "I am not a crook." Few people stopped to reflect that journalists had been asking the hard questions that prompted this reply, that an ordinary reporter had to face the leader of the most powerful nation in the world and ask him: "Well, *are* you a crook?" It is not a job for shrinking violets.

From time to time a journalist must also resort to craftiness. Take the Associated Press rewrite man assigned to interview a celebrity getting off a plane at the local airport. The AP man knew that the airport would be jammed with reporters and that getting to speak to the arriving VIP would be well-nigh impossible. Instead of joining the mob scene and trusting to his elbows to see him through, he stepped into a nearby telephone booth and called the airport message desk.

As the celebrity came off the plane, an announcement was made over the public address system asking him to "Come to the phone immediately." He did, ignoring the pushing, shoving knot of photographers and reporters in the arrivals lounge. It was the AP calling. The wire service reporter got the first interview, free of interruptions, and was able to go back to his bureau and put the story on the wire fifteen minutes ahead of his competition.

It goes without saying that the best reporters are naturally curious. Asking questions about a situation and finding the answers is what news gathering is all about. That curiosity, however, must be detached and objective. A journalist must be able to look at a disaster happening before his eyes, perhaps engulfing him, and separate from it the answers to the questions: "Who, what, when, where, and why?"

He must also be able, as far as humanly possible, to separate his own personal biases and opinions from his report of the facts. He must have a sense of fair play and be willing to give both sides in any controversy—including the side he doesn't agree with—their say.

This implies a measure of honesty on the reporter's part, something that ultimately rests on the journalist's religious or ethical system of values.

An unscrupulous journalist, particularly if he occupies an editor's position, can do enormous damage, spreading lies, propaganda, or misinformation born of mere carelessness. Misled by false or inaccurate news reports, the public can suffer greatly. It is important, then, that a journalist be a person whose personal beliefs are consistent with a high regard for truth and fair play.

An example of the effects of irresponsible reporting can be seen in the coverage two local papers gave to a brawl that took place after a high school basketball game in the suburbs of a large Midwestern U.S. city a few years ago. The brawl began when a group of white students from the host school began scuffling with a pair of black youths from the visiting school. Blacks in the gymnasium audience sided with the black students, whites with the whites, and a melee broke out. Police brought the actual fighting under control within a few minutes, but the real trouble had only begun.

A local weekly paper serving the black community wrote a story on the brawl, asserting that mobs of white adults had beaten black children and that police had turned vicious attack dogs on helpless students and their teachers. The weekly paper serving the white area where the host team's members lived also reported the story, stating that knife-wielding black students had started the brawl. The white community paper used derogatory language in its article, actually printing racial insults. Neither paper had had a reporter present at the scene.

The result of the stories was that both the white and black communities became enraged, racial hatred was inflamed all over the metropolitan area, and several games in the series had to be canceled for fear the students would kill each other if they were allowed to come together under one roof. The police had not used attack dogs (only one dog was present, a tracking dog that remained locked inside a police cruiser throughout the brawl) nor employed more force than needed to bring the disturbance under control. Nevertheless, for weeks afterward officers were subjected to accusations of racism and brutality. Support for high school sports in the community, particularly basketball, suffered a setback that took years to reverse. High school leagues all over the state were eventually affected.

The fact that a brawl involving several people had taken place was bad enough. But the fanning of the flames of racial hatred by the two newspapers involved made things many times worse. The brand of emotional, irresponsible reporting indulged in by their reporters and editors should have gotten them drummed out of the profession. Unfortunately, they are still in it.

Willing to Work

Managing editors are also looking for people who are willing to work hard, who will see a story through to completion even if it means logging a few overtime hours or putting in an extra effort beyond the routine grind.

Journalism is similar to police work. A good detective does not break off hot pursuit of a suspect promptly at five o'clock simply because his shift ends. The suspect might kill somebody or rob a bank while the policeman is punching his time clock. A reporter must often function the same way, continuing an interview, a file search, or a stakeout even past his dinner hour. Most news people are now union members, and their contracts with newspaper management set limits on the overtime hours they must work. But some overtime is required of every reporter if he or she wants to do the job right.

A would-be reporter should also be dependable. A harassed assignment editor counting on a reporter to come in and cover that last-minute press conference called by the mayor will be exceedingly annoyed if the reporter picks that day to arrive late. If a reporter promises to cover a story, he had better come through or he will be tossed out the front door rather abruptly.

Those with whom a reporter has made an appointment for an interview also tend to become irritated if the newsman doesn't show up. Too many such gaffes and a reporter may find himself without any sources for his stories. His reputation will get around, and people won't bother to talk to him.

Anxious to avoid getting stuck with a lemon on their staffs, managing editors would ideally like to hire only those who have had five years or more of reporting experience and who have repeatedly proven themselves in the business. This is feasible for some big-city dailies that always have many times more job applicants than there are jobs available. They can afford to be choosy.

In reality, however, most editors must lower their sights. They are willing to take on a beginner from time to time if only because they have no other choice.

When they do hire a green reporter, though, they try to minimize the risk. Those who have had formal university schooling are frequently preferred, because getting through a degree program shows, if nothing else, a certain amount of determination. In theory, it is also supposed to guarantee that the applicant has a basic knowledge of the shape of the society of which he is a part. Other qualifications, such as the ability to speak a foreign language or to type rapidly on deadline, are also looked upon with favor by those who do the hiring.

The applicants most likely to be hired, however, are those who show a potential for growth as human beings, as well as growth in the profession. The more lively and interested the applicant's personality, the more likely he or she is to survive and grow on the varied diet the business supplies to its practitioners. In the long haul such characteristics are to the employer's advantage, as well as to that of the individual reporter. They are more important, over the span of a person's career, than the amount of formal schooling with which he or she may have begun or the speed with which he or she may type or take shorthand. Mechanical skills, when needed, can be learned quickly, and the best schools are not always those accredited by the board of education.

CHAPTER V

Schools and Schools of Hard Knocks

The managing editor of the Edmonton (Alberta) *Sun* never went to a university. Now in complete charge of a major daily newspaper and earning a five-figure annual salary, he started in journalism at the bottom, as a "go-fer" copyboy, and worked his way up the ladder the hard way, learning on the job.

His achievement can still be repeated, but he and others like him would probably have found the going a lot easier if they'd had the benefit of more formal schooling.

Simply holding a degree in journalism is no guarantee that a person will get a reporting job, nor does it assure—as many editors have found to their chagrin—that the degree holder knows anything about the news business. Nevertheless, a hard-working, serious person who approaches schooling with a positive attitude can gain immeasurably from university or junior college training.

If a prospective journalist has the time (two to five years) and the money (several thousand dollars) to invest in post-secondary education, he should by all means make the investment. Virtually every university in the United States and Canada offers journalism or writing courses of some kind, and a degree in almost any subject can prove helpful in newspaper work.

Reference books such as the well-known *Barron's Guide* series, available in most school and public libraries, list colleges and universities in the United States and Canada, stating subjects taught and other information. *Barron's* produces separate guides for two-year and four-year institutions. Most colleges and universities also produce their own catalogs, which can be obtained by writing to the registrar.

The best-known journalism schools in the United States include the journalism faculty at Columbia University in New York, founded in

1912 and endowed by Joseph Pulitzer; the University of Missouri School of Journalism, founded in 1908; and the journalism faculty at the University of Wisconsin, opened in 1905. In Canada, the best-known journalism schools are those at Carleton University in Ottawa and at Ryerson Polytechnical Institute in Toronto.

The courses offered at most journalism schools today include a blend of liberal arts subjects such as history, literature, philosophy, and psychology, with practical subjects such as photography, composition, page layout, and elementary computer science. They are designed to make the student a well-rounded person, aware of the basic trends in society, but also possessed of the specialized skills needed in the newsroom.

Whether they succeed in reaching that goal has been the focus of heated debate. There is a sizeable body of working newsmen and women, many of whom are themselves journalism graduates, who insist that journalism schools do a wonderful job. But there is an equally sizeable group who are adamant that journalism schools are a waste of time and their graduates not worth two cents. In reality, the value of a journalism major depends on the quality of the school and that of the student. The academic excellence of a university faculty may vary widely from school to school and year to year, depending on its teachers. The effort and enthusiasm of their students are also as varied as the graduates are numerous.

The best journalism schools are those that give their students plenty of practice in actually gathering and writing news stories, either for a student newspaper, through free-lance assignments for local publications, or through part-time or summer internships on a daily newspaper.

One university journalism faculty, which charitably shall remain nameless, actually forbade its students to write for off-campus newspapers or magazines, on the theory that by doing so they might "pick up bad writing habits" not taught at the university. This policy was, of course, totally idiotic. *Any* practical experience, obtained anywhere, is of value to beginners in the craft. Preventing students from writing for a working publication was like explaining the backstroke to a class of swimmers and then refusing to let them go near the water.

People learn best by doing, whether in journalism or any other endeavor. All the university's policy did was retard the learning process for its pupils and make it more difficult for them to find jobs after graduation. Forbidden to free-lance, they had no clips of published stories to show prospective employers as proof of their ability. All they had were typed papers written as class assignments.

The student newspapers of many colleges and universities provide opportunities for journalism majors to gain reporting experience. Some university publications, such as the University of Michigan's *Michigan Daily* or Harvard University's *Harvard Crimson,* have earned reputations on their own for high quality. *The Michigan State News,* published by students at Michigan State University, actually functions in part as the local community newspaper for the city of East Lansing. Other student efforts, such as the famed *Harvard Lampoon,* have provided the inspiration for successful commercial publications. The popular satirical magazine *National Lampoon* can trace its antecedents to Harvard.

Not all student publications, obviously, are of such high quality, but even the most mediocre school paper gives its writers the opportunity to write for a public, on deadline. Such experience is worth a hundred classroom assignments.

Still more valuable are the intern, or work-study, programs available at some universities. These programs, established under the joint sponsorship of the school and participating newspapers, permit journalism students to spend the summer vacation working as reporters at a regular daily paper. After the three-month on-the-job training period, the students return to their classroom routine. The program has evident advantages for the schools and students involved, who gain irreplaceable experience. But it also has advantages for the newspaper. The students constitute extra bodies available for the assignment editor to call on during the summer months, when many of his regular staff are on vacation. The best of summer interns also represent a pool of talent available in future, when the newspaper is hiring.

An editor who has worked with a writer for three months over the summer will be more likely to hire that person full time than to hire a complete stranger, if for no other reason than that the student is a known quantity.

Sometimes, too, a summer student's ability can be so marked as to surprise the editors training him. One such student, working for a large daily, turned in a feature story on a local homosexual bar that was so well done it won the paper a national journalism award. The student won $1,000 for that story, and the paper hired him full time as a feature writer the following autumn.

A high school student planning to enter a university or junior college journalism program should prepare while still in secondary school by paying particular attention to courses in English grammar, literature, and composition and, when available, by taking elective courses in typing and shorthand, especially typing. A good grounding in history, social studies, and perhaps a foreign language is also helpful.

Other Majors

Journalism is not the only subject a prospective reporter can major in at a university. The city hall reporter at one major daily has a degree in city planning and administration. He knows more about running a city government than most elected officials, and his stories pointing out the officials' shortcomings keep the local party hacks hopping. The court reporter at the same newspaper has a prelaw degree, which he earned before he found out how hard it is to pass the Bar exams, and one of the reporters on the finance beat has a degree in economics.

A chemistry or biology major could prove valuable for a science writer, and a sports writer with a degree in physical education—especially if he played competitively for his university team—has a leg up on his rivals when it comes to understanding the sports beat.

We are living in an age of experts, and the combination of specialized knowledge with basic writing ability and a typing speed fast enough to meet deadlines can make a man or woman very valuable to a news gathering organization. Some newspapers and television networks put a premium on specialized knowledge and actually seek out graduates in areas where they plan to provide their readers or viewers with heavy coverage.

A literate engineering graduate with a good grounding in energy subjects would be invaluable to a newspaper trying to provide in-depth coverage of oil shortages, nuclear regulatory activities, and the development of solar and wind energy sources. A graduate who had majored in Russian or Polish language and literature and studied the history of Eastern Europe would be a natural candidate to man the Moscow bureau of a major news organization—provided, of course, that the graduate could write.

There are nearly as many beats on a modern newspaper as there are subjects in the modern university curriculum. Knowing this, the value of university study should be apparent, not only to job seekers but to newspaper publishers and editors as well. Many news people continue taking university courses even after they have begun working full-time for a newspaper or broadcast station. Larger newspapers now frequently pay for employees' tuition and arrange for them to take time off to attend courses that will make them more valuable on the job.

Besides ordinary journalism courses, many universities also offer majors in broadcast journalism, providing students with specialized training in the techniques of electronic news gathering. Students learn to write, direct, and produce television broadcasts and have the opportunity to see their work actually televised over university stations.

Two-year journalism courses, concentrating on strictly job-related courses, such as news story composition or page layout, and ignoring more general subjects such as history or literature, are also available at many community colleges with a trades orientation. Though much narrower in their focus, some of these programs are excellent within their limits, providing a practical alternative for those who do not have the time or cash to follow a full four-year university degree program.

University of Hard Knocks

North America's colleges and universities are not the only places where men or women can continue their education after high school. Real learning, in school or out, is self-administered. Teachers act mainly as catalysts, speeding up the process by which students discover things for themselves—and teachers in the school of hard knocks are found everywhere.

The outdoor writer at one big daily is a high school graduate who simply loves to hunt and fish. He never went to a university, but he worked as a fishing guide in a northern wilderness area, taking fishermen on canoe and backpack trips into the bush, flying wealthy executives into remote lakes in a seaplane, and teaching tourists the ways of the bushcraftsman.

At the suggestion of friends, he wrote a few free-lance articles based on his experiences as a guide and sent them to various publications to see if they would buy them. They did. In fact, one newspaper liked his work so much they gave him a contract to produce a regular column for its sports section. The column proved popular. He syndicated it, and it now appears in several newspapers and a magazine.

When he writes about the outdoors, readers sense immediately that he knows what he is talking about firsthand. They also sense his enthusiasm for his subject. That enthusiasm is genuine—he loves the woods and lakes of the north—and establishes a rapport with any audience.

Working as a guide, the columnist learned many lessons, not all of which were pleasant. He found, for example, that some of the wealthy, powerful men he flew to remote lakes to fish were less interested in the sport than they were in the prestige of being able to tell their friends and business associates what great sportsmen they were. Often, the fish they had mounted on the wall of the den at home had been caught by the guide, not the fisherman. They had no real love for the outdoors, nor any concern for preserving it.

Others were the opposite. Weary of the hectic pace of their high-pressure jobs, they found the peace of the woods an immense relief. They loved every minute of their trip in the bush and became keen—and honest—sportsmen. The guide's job, in short, taught him a lot about human nature and how the general public looks on the natural world. The lessons were valuable ones and made his columns, which reflected his knowledge, that much more interesting to read.

Another great reporter, Dennis Smith, received his education as a member of the New York City Fire Department, where he risked life and limb for many years before it occurred to him that he ought to write a book about what he had been living through. The book, *Report from Engine Company 82,* was a masterpiece of straight journalism, recounting in graphic detail the hard, yet immensely rewarding, life of a fire fighter in a major American city. Smith now contributes regularly to a magazine for fire fighters and is considered by many firemen to be their journalistic spokesman, embodying their lives and dreams in print.

Perhaps even more unusual is the society reporter for *Esquire* magazine, Taki Theodoracopulos, who writes a column called "High Life" under the by-line Taki. The son of a Greek shipping magnate who was once prime minister of Greece, Theodoracopulos was born rich. He went to exclusive prep schools, dabbled in semi-pro tennis, and has mixed all his life with the international jet set.

He could have gone into the family shipping business but, according to his editors at *Esquire,* preferred journalism. The subject he eventually ended up covering was the one he knew best from personal experience: high society.

"Being rich myself, and being extremely conservative in my politics, I hate the irresponsible rich, the tax exiles, people who hide their money in Liechtenstein and do nothing except try to beat the system. I believe very much in the responsibility of the aristocracy," Taki once told an interviewer. His columns, in which the "irresponsible rich" are sliced verbally into shreds, reflect his sense of journalistic mission.

The outdoorsman, the fire fighter, and the chronicler of high society all had two things in common. They wrote about what they knew best, and they didn't go to journalism school to learn to do it.

Another reporter, now covering city hall in a large northeastern city, went to school but spent only the barest minimum of time there. He took a one-year crash course in journalism at a local community college and then got a job on a suburban weekly newspaper. The stories he wrote for the weekly were so well done that the editor of the city's morning daily paper noticed them and hired him.

The time this reporter spent on the weekly was not very well paid; in fact, his pay was close to the starvation level for a married man, which he was. But it was time well spent because he learned what he had to know and, in the end, got the job he wanted.

Writing in Journalese

Among the things the city hall reporter, and every other journalist, must learn is the curious art of writing in "journalese," the specialized style of communication unique to journalism. It is a style of writing not taught in standard English composition courses, but it is admirably suited to its purpose, namely, to recount the greatest number of relevant facts in the fewest number of words and with the greatest amount of attraction possible for the reader. The style has taken hundreds of years to develop, and it is still changing.

Feature writers and columnists, of course, strive to develop a personal writing style and generally do not write in journalese. But even the most unorthodox of feature writers had to serve an apprenticeship somewhere, and more than likely it was on a beat doing "straight news" stories—the matter-of-fact, unadorned reports that fill most of the news columns in a paper. Ninety-nine percent of these are written in journalese.

Learning journalese is not terribly difficult. An enterprising writer can teach himself by getting a good journalism textbook from the library and studying it, then practicing at home or writing free-lance articles. Even if no one buys the articles, the practice obtained in writing them will be worthwhile.

"Leads" are basic to this kind of writing. A lead is the first or leading paragraph of a newspaper story. It is the most important paragraph, because the reader sees it first and decides then whether he'll bother to keep on reading. If the reader is pressed for time and cannot finish reading the entire story, he should be able to get all of the basic facts about it from the lead alone.

A good lead should be interesting enough to snare attention while at the same time answering "the five W's and one H," namely "who, what, where, when, why, and how." In short, it summarizes the story. Here's an example:

> A 17-year-old youth was shot and killed yesterday when grocer Mark Lucas, 44, fired a shotgun at a fleeing bandit on Market Street, missing the bandit but hitting a passing school bus.

Who? Mark Lucas. What? Killed a 17-year-old youth. When? Yesterday. Where? On Market Street. Why? Because he was trying to hit a bandit. How? With a shotgun.

A close look at most of the news stories in a daily newspaper will reveal a similar pattern. In the example given, the fact that a 17-year-old youth was shot to death was unusual enough in itself to attract the attention of readers. The additional fact that the youth's name was not given in the first paragraph is also likely to hold their attention for at least a few more lines. They will want to know who the victim was. Perhaps he was a neighbor or even a relative. This information would normally be in the second paragraph, which might say:

> "Oh God, what have I done?" sobbed grocer Lucas when told that his shot had fatally wounded young Lenny Martens, a passenger on the school bus. Martens, the only son of Mr. and Mrs. Jack Martens of suburban Warren, was the star quarterback on the Central High School varsity football team.

There are other ways of writing a lead, of course. Sometimes the reporter deliberately puts off answering the five W's and one H until the second or third paragraph, choosing instead to use the "teaser lead." Here is an example of teaser technique:

> "When the window glass broke at first I thought somebody had thrown a rock at the bus. Then I saw Lenny fall over in his seat and I screamed. He was all bloody."
> Tears still streaming down her face, 16-year-old Mary Franklin used these words yesterday to describe the death of a classmate on a fateful bus ride that no one at Central High School will ever forget.
> It was the ride on which young Lenny Martens, 17, fell victim

to the poor aim and reckless bravado of a local grocer, who fired a shotgun at a fleeing bandit and killed Central's athlete of the year."

In this lead, the writer has counted on the obvious drama contained in the 16-year-old girl's quotes to attract and hold the readers' attention. Not until the third paragraph does the writer provide answers to the basic questions of the straight news lead.

Both types of lead are acceptable in straight news writing, but in general the teaser lead is used less often. It is extremely rare to find a nonfeature story in which the five W's and one H are answered any later than the third paragraph.

As for the rest of the straight news story, it generally follows the "pyramid" structure. The lead paragraph, summarizing the bare details of the event, is compared to the point of a pyramid. Spreading out from it on both sides is the body of the story, which gradually widens the readers' understanding of an event by providing more detail, quotes, and description as it progresses.

The most important or the most recent developments in the story are described first, the less important ones afterward, in a descending order of priority. Frequently, although not always, the story is completed by a "kicker" line, used by the writer as a sort of parting shot at the end.

There are many other rules in news writing. For example, if an article involves a highly controversial subject and one of the persons being quoted is strongly partisan, the reporter generally tries to get a comment from someone with an opposing view to balance the story. The quotes from one spokesman or woman are given, then those of the opposing side are reported in the paragraph immediately following. If a person is being accused of wrongdoing, his words in defending himself or answering the charges against him are generally given immediately after the paragraph stating the accusation. Here is an example:

Alderman John Brinks has been arrested and charged with accepting a bribe following the report to police that a local building contractor paid Brinks $5,000 shortly before being granted a contract to construct an addition to City Hall.

"This is all a terrible mistake. I'm being framed by my political enemies," an indignant Brinks told newsmen this morning as he walked, handcuffed, up the stairs to his cell at the County Jail.

Failure to give an accused person a chance to defend himself, or to balance the remarks of a partisan spokesman with those of his opponents, can seriously weaken the credibility of a news story. To deliberately write stories with such weaknesses is to indulge in mere propaganda.

The pyramid style of story construction has evolved over the years as a result primarily of efforts to capture and hold reader interest, particularly the interest of readers who may be in a hurry and who lack time to read a long article at a leisurely pace. But reader interest wasn't the only concern of those who helped develop the style. The convenience of copy editors, makeup editors, and printers was also a factor.

The pyramid style article puts the most important facts first, the least important details last. This means that if the story turns out to be too long to fit in the space available on a given page it can be cut easily from the bottom. Told by a printer that a story is six inches too long, a copy editor can simply trim six inches worth of any pyramid story from the end and know that the essential details are still intact in the earlier paragraphs. On deadline, this saves a great deal of agony. (The length of newspaper stories is measured not in words, but in inches, that is, the actual length of a story, measured with a ruler, when it has been set in type in column form.)

Copy editors, particularly the older ones who are suspicious of stylistic innovations of any kind, usually hate to be asked to cut the work of feature writers. They know that many feature writers do not follow the pyramid style, and as a result important facts and key quotes may be scattered throughout the story rather than bunched together in the first few paragraphs. In order to "chop" such a story without leaving out something important, the copy editor must read it through completely, and sometimes actually rewrite it himself, before deleting anything. That takes time, and when the clock's hands are nearing deadline time is precious.

"Wire copy," that is, stories written by the wire services such as AP or UPI, is generally a perfect example of pyramid style writing. The authors of these stories know their work will be distributed over the teleprinters to newsrooms all over the world and that each newspaper will have different amounts of space available. A 20-inch story from the AP Cleveland bureau may appear in the Cleveland *Plain Dealer* still 20 inches long. The same story in the San Francisco *Chronicle* may rate only five paragraphs. An AP writer accordingly makes certain all the important facts are contained in those first five paragraphs.

Journalists who write for broadcast stations, whether television or radio, also have to learn a specialized style of expression. As mentioned in Chapter I, their news "splits" are measured in seconds, rather than inches, that is, the number of seconds it would take a broadcaster to read them aloud into the microphone.

Generally, broadcast writing is deliberately conversational in tone, for the simple reason that the broadcaster *is* conversing with his listeners. Contractions ("isn't," rather than "is not") and slang expressions are much more frequent in broadcast stories, and the storytelling or anecdotal abilities of the writer are stressed.

There are many other specialized skills that apprentice newsmen or women must learn before they can call themselves professionals. Some skills, like typing, shorthand, or the operation of a video display computer terminal, are purely mechanical. They are taught as part of the curriculum at most journalism schools, but those who have not taken a journalism major can still pick them up in actual practice during their first month or two on the job.

Typing, of course, is rather fundamental, but even this skill can sometimes be acquired at the last minute. The education reporter for one major daily paper did not know how to type when he was hired. The editor who hired him simply assumed he could type, and the reporter was not about to tell him differently. In a frantic burst of energy, he spent an entire weekend going over and over the lessons in a Gregg typing manual. His speed by Monday morning was still dismal, and when deadline time arrived he still hadn't finished typing his very first story for the paper.

Desperate, he gave up trying to learn the touch system and resorted to typing with one finger—the index finger of his right hand. His arm was a veritable blur as he typed, but he got the story done. The habit of typing with one finger stuck, and for years afterward he continued to type that way. Eventually, he worked his speed up to about 50 words per minute on one finger, an incredible feat. Visitors to the newsroom would often do a double-take when they saw him at his desk, rapping away with one hand at the keyboard. One of his nicknames among his fellow reporters was "Lone Finger."

Page layout, the art of making stories fit on a given newspaper page and arranging them in a pattern pleasing enough to the reader's eye to make him want to read them, is another skill that can be acquired on the job. It is closely related to the basic artistic skill of composition, the same skill utilized by photographers and fine artists in deciding on the arrangement of objects in their pictures. Often a good makeup editor is also a good amateur photographer or Sunday painter. The mentality of the disciplines is similar.

Intangible Skills

Some things, of course, cannot be taught in schools, and some things cannot be taught at all. Sensitivity to the subtle differences in personality between people, the knack for gaining others' confidence, an eye for details, and the ability to spot the significant point in a welter of otherwise useless information—none of these things can be imparted in the classroom. They can only be acquired through actual experience in life.

The person who is born with the native ability to learn these things quickly, who operates, as the saying goes, "with his antennae out" at all times, is the kind of person who will succeed in journalism. If that person is also curious and has an innate "nose for news," he or she may have the makings of an outstanding journalist.

First, however, a would-be reporter must find an editor who is hiring and persuade that editor to hire *him*. Like any salesman pushing a product—in this case himself—the job applicant should start by getting his foot in the door.

CHAPTER VI

Your Foot in the Door

Obviously, a newcomer with no practical experience is going to get a fast trip to the nearest exit if he or she walks into the newsroom of a big daily like the Washington *Post* or the Chicago *Tribune* and asks for a reporting job.

You may think you are God's gift to journalism, but that managing editor couldn't care less. He wants experienced people, people who have the credentials to prove they already know how to do the job. On a major metropolitan daily, that generally means people with a minimum of three to five years of experience, or writers who have already sold the paper several free-lance articles that the editor liked and that graphically demonstrated the applicants' abilities.

Where does a person get experience and/or free-lance credits?

Several places. A university or community college graduate, of course, might have written articles for a student newspaper or magazine, or for journalism writing courses, and these can be submitted when applying for work to demonstrate what the applicant has done. Far better than writing for a school paper or on assignment from a professor, however, is proof of actual writing for a regular newspaper or magazine, for a weekly paper, a small-town daily, or the trade press.

A good route to follow, tried by many successful news people and found reliable, is as follows. Make the rounds of all of the weekly papers, small town dailies, and trade papers within striking distance and try for full-time work at each one. If no full-time work is available, try for a part-time job. If there are no part-time openings, ask the editors if they are in the market for free-lance work and, if so, what subjects are of most interest to them.

If Lady Luck is smiling, this initial foray may net a full-time job immediately. If not, go home and get out the typewriter. The editors will have stated what kind of free-lance articles they are buying. Write one. Sell it, and then write another one. An editor who likes a writer's free-lance work will call that writer before anyone else when a job opening crops up on his paper. He'll already know the writer, know his or her ability, and know that he or she wants the job badly enough to keep coming back.

Once you get a full-time job on a small publication, you'll pile up experience fast. Weeklies and trade publications are generally short-staffed, which means you'll probably write your fingers off. You'll also start to meet people, to make contacts who may prove valuable in getting a better job later on. If you cover a county board of supervisors meeting for a weekly, you may find the government reporter for a nearby daily paper at the same meeting. Introduce yourself.

The reporting fraternity is gregarious. The daily reporter may tell you when an opening crops up at his paper. If he likes you and your work, he may even put in a good word for you with his boss if you decide to apply for the job. You'll also be piling up clippings of your published work, with your name in the by-line to show potential employers.

Then again, you may not want to leave the weekly or trade paper. You may decide you eventually want to be the editor of it, rather than a mere reporter, or even to buy it someday and become a publisher yourself. Such things happen. The editor or publisher of a weekly paper may make as much as a reporter on a major daily. It is possible to choose between being the big fish in a small pond and a little fish in a big one.

The important thing is to be persistent, to keep coming back, and to keep writing, writing, writing. Eventually it *will* pay off. Every by-line, no matter where it appears, brings an apprentice a step closer to a successful career.

The Want-ads

Large dailies and the major wire services rarely advertise job openings, preferring to fill them through word of mouth and personal contacts. However, small and medium-sized publications, including the country weeklies, small-town dailies, and trade publications where a beginner stands the best chance of being hired, do advertise.

The best place to look for such advertisements is in *Editor & Publisher* magazine, whose classified advertising section is read by more reporters and editors than that of any other trade journal. *E&P,* as it is known in the business, is published weekly from offices at 575 Lexington Ave., New York, NY 10022. It contains both a "Help Wanted" section, where employers advertise job openings, and a "Positions Wanted" section, where reporters and editors make their availability known. From time to time even the large publications place advertisements in *E&P,* although this does not happen often.

The cost of placing an advertisement in the "Positions Wanted" section is not high, and those who wish to keep their identity confidential (for fear their present boss will find out they are job-hunting) can use a box number for replies rather than give their name and address. *E&P* forwards letters sent to one of its box numbers to the privacy-seeking advertiser, without divulging the advertiser's name.

A similar classified advertising service is offered by the Canadian trade magazine *Content,* published from offices at 91 Raglan Ave., Toronto, Ontario, Canada M6C 2K7.

The reporters and editors who advertise in *E&P* spend considerable time deciding exactly how to word their advertisements, and with good reason. Even those who employ classified ads to sell mere objects, such as used cars or camera equipment, word their ads with care. But *E&P*'s advertisers are actually selling their writing ability, and they strive to make their ads show it to advantage.

Sometimes they overdo it. A daily advertising for a new city editor may try to appear official and important—"Big Time"—in its ad and succeed only in making itself look pompous and stuffy. A young reporter attempting to project a false image of experience may only make himself look cynical and conniving. Like the best news writing, the best ads are simple and direct. They state what the advertiser has to offer and what he hopes to find with no frills or efforts to coin puns and fancy phrases. An example is this ad, placed by a journalism graduate with one year's experience on a suburban weekly:

HARD-WORKING CUB, J-grad, one year doing everything on suburban weekly, seeks chance to learn and grow on a daily. Will travel. Box 1711, *Editor & Publisher.*

This is plain, straightforward writing and makes no attempt to hide the job-seeker's beginner status. It makes clear that he or she is determined and willing to work, and an employer reading the ad would be happy to note the phrase "seeks chance to learn." This indicates that the cub in question is not a wiseacre who thinks he knows it all. Chances are that the writer of this advertisement will get several serious replies from editors seeking general assignment reporters.

Free lancers seeking spot or one-time story assignments also advertise in *Editor & Publisher.*

Even if you are not planning on advertising for a job right away, it may be worthwhile to obtain a copy of *E&P* from the library and read over its classified section. It will provide a valuable glimpse into the mentality of those on both sides of the fence in the journalistic job market.

Often beginning journalists, whether reading *E&P's* classified ads or talking to someone in the business, hear of a publication looking for staff but decline to apply for the job on grounds that the paper or magazine in question is beneath their notice. A cub with dreams of glory, imagining himself grilling presidents and prime ministers, will automatically reject the chance to go to work for *The Box and Bag News* or *The Grocery Journal.*

By so doing, he may be throwing away his best chance of breaking into the business. The big-time daily will likely not hire an inexperienced person, and those who turn up their noses at the small-time jobs available may end up with nothing. Besides, some trade journals are very well written, perform a useful function in society, and maintain high professional standards. *Automotive News,* the journal of the automobile industry, is an excellent example. This paper, published in Detroit, consistently produces expertly researched, objective, in-depth reports on the auto industry. It is read thoroughly by the auto and business editors of every major North American publication and has published so many major scoops that many writers on daily papers envy its record. A beginner could do a lot worse than to find a job with such a publication. Indeed, he or she would be lucky to find one there.

The only jobs a beginner should turn down are those that would require him to indulge in obscenity, libel, or public relations work.

Writing obscenities and publishing libel are illegal. Public relations work is not, but it might as well be as far as the effect it can have on a journalist's reputation is concerned. Tarring an entire profession because of the bad actions of some of its members is, of course, unfair. There are many men and women in public relations who do an honest and effective job. But journalists, fairly or not, almost invariably regard those they disparagingly call "PR flacks" as among the lowest of species.

Having worked in public relations can actually be considered a strike against a young job-hunter, rather than a point in favor.

The basis for journalists' low opinion of "flacks" is the knowledge that public relations people are paid to represent their clients or employers before the public, and that usually involves presenting the client or employer's good points and minimizing the bad. In other words, by its very nature, public relations writing is biased. News writers are often biased themselves, but don't like to admit it. To them objectivity is—quite rightly—sacrosanct. Their work is the very antithesis of public relations work: hence the instinctive dislike of flacks. In addition, a fair number of newsmen and women, after working for newspapers for several years, succumb to the lure of higher pay offered by the public relations departments of some large corporations. They switch jobs and, knowing their former co-workers look down on them for doing so, try to play the game of oneupmanship by boasting of their new salaries. The newspaper people become jealous and resentful of the boasting tone. Mutual mistrust and disgust inevitably grow.

Unless a young writer has decided on a career of public relations, he or she will be better off to stay away from such jobs. PR and news writing simply do not mix.

Query Letters and Résumés

A would-be reporter looking for work should apply in person at newspapers or magazines in his immediate area but obviously cannot very easily pay personal calls on publications in other cities, states, or provinces. Long-distance job-hunting requires the use of a well-written query letter and résumé. For that matter, a letter and résumé should also precede an applicant's first visit to a local paper.

A good query letter is as difficult to write as any newspaper story. Reading it, prospective employers get their first glimpse of the applicant's writing style and organizational ability, as well as the factual details of his or her educational background, previous job experience, and reasons for seeking the job in question.

Obviously, if the applicant wants a job, the query letter must be an example of clear, compact prose, free of digression and getting straight to the point. It should be written in much the same way that a good straight news story is composed, taking the first paragraph as the lead and developing the letter the way you would develop an article.

Some job applicants write their query letter as if it were a feature story, larding it with color, jokes, smart remarks, and devices intended to jolt an employer to get his attention. Only one in a hundred of these efforts manages to avoid sounding strained or forced, and the vast majority create a poor impression. It is much better to write in a friendly but businesslike tone and to avoid trying to show off.

That a query letter should be typed, double-spaced, rather than handwritten, goes without saying.

Here is an example of the first paragraph of a query letter that resulted in a personal interview being granted by a managing editor and eventually landed its author a job:

> I am a newsman with six years' experience writing and editing for daily newspapers and a wire service and am interested in the possibility of employment as a reporter or copy editor at *The County Times.*

The author of this letter is an experienced feature writer with a style of his own, but he did not attempt to "featurize" his job-seeking effort. The letter was blunt and matter-of-fact—and it worked.

Most managing editors are also blunt and matter-of-fact.

The second paragraph of the letter noted that a résumé of the writer's background was attached, and that résumé, also, was blunt and matter-of-fact. In outline form, it stated the applicant's name, age, address, marital status, and other vital statistics, then proceeded to list, chronologically, the schools he had attended, jobs he had held, and persons who could be contacted for personal references.

Also included in the envelope with the query letter and résumé were Xerox copies of two of the writer's more recent published news stories. One of them was a feature story in which the writer's unique style was given full rein, the other a straight news account to show that the author could handle both types of writing.

The query letter, typed double-spaced on one page, was eight paragraphs long, long enough to introduce the author but short enough to be read in a few seconds by a busy editor. Anything more than a single page of copy would probably not be read by someone in a hurry, so writing a longer letter would be a waste of time.

The letter was positive in nature, free of "negative vibes," and avoided stating why the writer was leaving his current job. Most people quit jobs because they dislike them, or dislike their boss, but saying so in a letter to another prospective boss is generally bad policy. It is better to give your reasons for leaving the old job only if requested to give them, and preferably only during a personal interview where you can explain what happened in detail.

A résumé can be photocopied, but query letters are generally typed individually and signed by hand for each prospective employer to whom they are sent. Some beginning journalists have sent letters and résumés to as many as 200 publications before finding a job, which means the applicant may get pretty tired of retyping the same query letter over and over. There is, unfortunately, no other way to do it. Managing editors don't want to feel they are getting a form letter. Even if they know it isn't true, they like job applicants to give the impression that the only paper they are applying to—the only one they would ever dream of applying to—is the one where this particular managing editor works. Getting work is rarely easy. Usually, finding a job is a job in itself.

Employment Interviews

If a query letter results in a request from a managing editor to come to his office for a personal interview, the job-hunter has won half the battle. A daily newspaper or broadcast station receives hundreds of job applications every year, sometimes hundreds a month, but the writers of only one or two are selected for a personal interview. The fact that your letter has prompted an interview means that the paper or station is very interested in your qualifications, and there is a good chance that you will be hired.

Getting an interview, however, does not guarantee a job. You can still muff it.

As already noted, an editor seeking reporting staff is unlikely to hire anyone who comes across as sloppy, unkempt, and boorish. Someone who acts like a rude clod in a job interview would probably act the same way if he or she were sent out to interview the mayor, a prospect the editor would like to avoid. At the same time, no editor is likely to hire someone who appears excessively shy and self-effacing, who mumbles, stutters, or simply sits blankly waiting for the other person in the room to say something.

A reporter must be able to initiate a conversation, keep it moving without difficulty, and at the same time be aggressive in seeking answers to his questions—politely aggressive, but aggressive nevertheless. The job of a journalist, after all, is to meet people from all walks of life, establish a rapport with them, and persuade them to provide information. It is a highly social form of work, and those who perform it must be highly sociable.

The best way to handle a job interview is probably to approach it as if it were a story interview—in other words, as if you were actually on a reporting assignment. Dress neatly, conduct yourself in a friendly but businesslike manner, and, as you would in a story interview, take your cues from the person being interviewed. If the editor seems in a hurry, don't take all day to come to the point. If he seems relaxed and grateful for a break, slow down yourself and take time for a bit of small talk.

You will, of course, have to answer several questions about your background, experience, goals, and hopes, but don't allow the interview to degenerate to the point where the editor asks all the questions and all you do is meekly reply. He is, after all, looking for a reporter who will dig out the news. Ask the editor a few questions of your own. Draw *him* out. If he's good at his job, he'll notice this and mark it down as a point in your favor. If he isn't good at his job, he'll take no notice and at least you will have lost nothing by your inquisitiveness. A job-hunter has a legitimate right to ask questions of a prospective employer, such as what kind of pay is being offered, what is required by the job, when a new employee would be expected to start, and so forth. So don't be shy; speak up.

Above all, do not try to put on an act, whether of phony sophistication or overeagerness. This is deadly. One editor, conducting a series of job interviews with university students, was absolutely amazed at the performance put on by a certain young man. Apparently, this poor creature had either imagined or been taught that the manners and mannerisms of the English upper class were a model for the world. His parents, the interviewing editor later discovered, were only one generation removed from Britain and were, indeed, well-to-do. Perhaps they had sent their son to a prep school, and that was where he had picked up his sad delusions.

At any rate, the young man, though born and raised in North America, was trying desperately to imitate, or impersonate, an Oxford don. He came to the interview wearing a tweed suit with leather patches on the jacket elbows and puffing an expensive briar pipe filled with Dunhill's Royal Yacht Tobacco. He smiled condescendingly and sat down, without being asked, in the chair opposite the editor and, in a studious imitation of an Oxford drawl, said: "How d'you do." It was unbelievable, a truly surreal experience.

A journalism teacher who could provide a reference was referred to as "a nice chap, actually," while one who had not provided any recommendation was put down as "a crashing bore." When this young man left shortly afterward, saying "cheerio" as he went out the door, the editor could only shake his head in disbelief. Needless to say, he did not get a job offer.

The applicant who did get that job was a young woman who came into the interview dressed in a businesslike sweater and skirt, carrying a pad and ballpoint pen with which, at one point in the interview, she actually took some notes. She introduced herself quickly, smiled, sat down, and awaited the first of the editor's questions. She had a clear, forthright answer for every one, asked several of her own, and before many minutes had passed had drawn the editor into a conversation on his *own* first efforts to find a job. She was friendly, relaxed, and obviously extremely intelligent and had a knack of putting people at ease.

She had pinned a button to her sweater that bore the legend "We try harder," and she gave the impression throughout the encounter that, indeed, she would try harder to get a story than any other student interviewed. She followed up the already highly favorable first impression made in this interview with subsequent letters and phone calls asking the editor whether any decisions had been made. She got the job.

Today, she is covering the social services beat on a major metropolitan daily newspaper, and she recently won a prestigious national journalism award. She deserved it.

The job-hunting odyssey of a second young woman is worth recounting, if only to show what the word "persistent" really means. This woman, a journalism school graduate, had had no luck finding work in her home town and had received no positive replies to the query letters she had sent to out-of-town employers. Many people would have given up at this point, but she didn't. She decided to follow up every one of the query letters she'd written with a personal visit to the newspapers involved, until one of them gave her a job or she ran out of newspapers.

She had mailed a lot of query letters to papers all over the United States, and the resulting trip, made on a shoestring budget, lasted several months. She took buses, trains, walked, and hitched rides all over the nation—but in the end was still jobless. A lesser person would have despaired.

But not this girl. She wrote a free-lance story about her trip and sold it to *Editor & Publisher,* and eventually one of those who read it hired her.

Imagine what a bulldog she would be in getting a story!

There are other ways to get a writing job than by applying for work as a reporter. The young woman mentioned in Chapter II, who eventually became a television newscaster, started out as a receptionist at a daily newspaper. Other journalists have started as proofreaders, copyboys, even building guards, just to get their foot in the door and get to know more about the business.

Working at a newspaper or broadcast station gives a job-hunter the chance to meet people from the news departments, perhaps at lunch or over a beer after work, and to hear of openings. One young woman who worked as a proofreader at a magazine was an avid gardener. When a local newspaper editor, who visited the magazine often, mentioned that he was looking for a gardening columnist, the proofreader volunteered. Her column now appears regularly in a weekly supplement to the paper, with her by-line prominent on it.

Another young man was working as a copyboy at a large daily, and after several years had not been able to get a reporting job. He had, however, come to know most of the newsmen and women in town and become very familiar with the in-house gossip of the profession. The publisher of a trade journal on the newspaper business hired him as a local "stringer" or correspondent, supplying him with news on the profession itself and the doings of its practitioners in that particular city.

The broadcasting industry is full of similar tales, in which office boys, researchers, and others work their way into a reporting job by being in the right place at the right time—and by being persistent.

Persistence is perhaps the most important quality required to find a job in journalism. It is a fascinating profession, with a slightly romantic aura about it in the public mind, and its members are fairly well paid. That means that a lot of people want to enter the business, and the competition for jobs is bound to be strong.

As already noted, the largest daily papers and most television stations receive hundreds of applications from would-be reporters every year, and only a small percentage of them are hired. The same is true of free-lance manuscripts sent in by hopeful writers. Perhaps one in fifty has a chance of actually being published.

The people who find jobs, and those whose articles get published, are the ones who keep coming back, who refuse to give up and take the first "no" for an answer. The saying "Don't give up before the fifth try," applies to job-hunting in the field of journalism. You might even add to it by trying a sixth time, especially if management has changed since the last attempt. Perhaps a managing editor at the same paper will hire you although his predecessor would not.

If you are trying to sell free-lance articles, the same rules apply. If the first publication to which you send a story rejects it, send it to another one and think up a new story idea for the first. Eventually something will click somewhere.

The law of averages favors repetition.

CHAPTER VII

On the Job

Cub reporters starting their first newspaper jobs are usually put on general assignment for at least a few months. This enables the editors to weigh each beginner's performance in a variety of situations and get an idea of where he or she ought to be permanently assigned. It also allows newcomers to sharpen their news-gathering skills while observing more experienced reporters in action, sizing up each job in the newsroom and deciding which they would like to shoot for as an eventual specialty.

A newsroom presents a wide variety of choices.

The police reporter, for example, usually walks around with an electronic pager clipped to his belt and spends a good deal of his time hunched over the paper's shortwave radio set, listening to the traffic on police frequencies. In some states tuning in to a police radio frequency is illegal, but virtually every major daily has such a set and, illegal or not, its reporters listen to police calls. They wear the portable pagers because police stories, unlike those on many other beats, do not confine themselves to business hours. A shooting, a hostage incident, or a prison break is as likely to occur at three in the morning as between the hours of nine to five, and the reporter must be available in case a hot one breaks.

Police reporters also tend to spend a good deal of time in the company of the paper's best spot news photographers, for the simple reason that they work together frequently and usually end up becoming friends. Both the police reporters and spot news photographers tend to be rather fast drivers and usually know the layout of the city's streets as well as most taxi drivers. Other reporters refer to the police beat people as "cop shop" reporters and sometimes, a bit condescendingly, as "cowboys" or "gonzos."

The best police reporters deserve the "cowboy" name, but as a compliment, not a form of reproach. They are people who deliberately seek trouble, thrive on it, and live for it. They are happiest when in motion, chasing or being chased, and detest routine. The police beat is the natural place for them. A good deal of their work, like that of any beat, *is* routine, but sooner or later that routine is bound to be broken. The moment the cop-shop cowboy lives for arrives.

It may be a hostage incident in which a trapped holdup man, caught

A cameraman prepares to shoot page one of a daily paper; from the photo will be made the plastic version of the page that will be used in printing (photo by Thomas Pawlick).

red-handed by police, tries to avoid capture at the last moment by taking hostages and holding them at gunpoint. Usually, such situations end in stalemates, with the police unwilling to attack for fear the hostages will be hurt, and the bandit unable to escape because the police have him surrounded.

In one such situation in Montreal, the holdup man refused to give up, and it wasn't until a local police reporter, Claude Poirier, was called to the scene and offered to act as a negotiator that the stalemate was broken. Poirier acted as a neutral go-between for the police and the bandit and eventually helped talk the holdup man into giving himself up. The resulting story was carried in papers all over the continent, and Poirier had an instant reputation. From then on, every time a group of holdup men took hostages, Poirier was called to negotiate. He became, through experience, an expert in hostage negotiations, and police in many cities came to seek his advice.

Every time he entered a bank or store where a panicky gunman held a hostage, Poirier was risking his own life. But this kind of thing is what the best police reporters thrive upon, and it makes for fascinating reading.

The plain fact is that police stories, particularly those that involve violent crime, are dramatic, and newspaper readers love drama. Put the words "murder," "Mafia," or "chase" in a headline, and the story under it is virtually guaranteed to be read.

The police reporter's search for authentic detail and the drama of crime make him strive to be the first on the scene, available to get the fresh quote or description that will make a story come alive. Sometimes a reporter may beat the police to the scene of a crime, such as the time when a young Detroit reporter heard an announcement over the police radio that "A holdup is in progress at the White Tower hamburger stand at Woodward and Pittfield." The reporter and photographer jumped in one of the big, red V-8 station wagons provided by their paper and roared off to the address given, at one point actually driving down a deserted sidewalk to avoid a traffic tie-up.

They arrived at the scene ahead of the police and walked into the hamburger stand cautiously. Inside, a huge, fat waitress in a white uniform was standing behind the counter, looking as if nothing at all had happened. " 'Lo," she said casually.

"Is this the place where there was a holdup?" the reporter asked, uncertain that they had come to the right address.

"Uh-huh!" said the waitress. "This is the place all right!" She chuckled good-naturedly and jerked her thumb in the direction of the floor behind the counter. There, face down under the open cash register drawer, lay the would-be bandit, dead as a stone, a huge butcher knife sticking out of his back and his gun, unfired, still in his hand.

"He weren't very smart," the waitress said. "I got him when he turned his back." She calmly poured three cups of coffee, assuming that the newsmen were police there to take her statement, then asked as an afterthought: "I suppose you boys 'd like a burger, too?"

When homicide detectives did arrive, the reporter and photographer were already leaving, both astounded at the waitress' calm, but ecstatic at the story they had to report.

Of course, such incidents do not happen every day, or even every month, on the police beat. Many large dailies have also adopted a policy of playing down police and crime news, so that the story mentioned above might not even be reported in their news pages. Other papers publish crime news in digest form, printing only a brief article noting that, say, six holdups took place in the city that day, in which bandits stole X number of dollars. The theory behind this policy is that giving attention to violent crime only gives ideas to those who read about it, and that crime stories also take up space in the paper that could be devoted to issues of greater importance.

Papers that still regularly cover crime news counter that crime is important to their readers, who may become its victims at any time, and that human interest stories are what sell newspapers. Probably both sides in the controversy have a point. Overdone, crime stories are no more than cheap sensationalism, but at the same time the existence of crime cannot be ignored. It is part of the news and should be covered, not covered up.

The police reporter, with his intimate knowledge of the daily work life of police officers, is also best qualified to handle the in-depth coverage of such subjects as a city's police budget, labor negotiations between police and their civilian management, and the wider social causes and effects of crime. Prison reform, compensation of crime victims by government, and other issues also fall under his purview. When the police reporter is not "out chasing squad cars," there is still plenty to keep him occupied. Of all those on the staff of a daily newspaper, the police reporter probably logs the most overtime.

Almost as busy, at least in a large city, are the city hall and labor beats. The reporters who cover these beats rarely have time to twiddle their thumbs. Usually they come to the office early to check for mail and telephone messages. Then, after informing the assignment editor where they plan to spend their shift, they go out and start pounding the pavement.

The city hall reporter begins making the rounds of his or her contacts in city government: politicians, secretaries, contractors doing business with the city, the heads of citizens' groups and voter blocs. Meetings of the City Council, the Zoning Board, and all sorts of committees must be covered. In the morning, the beat man gets copies of the agenda for each meeting, phones or goes in person to see those who will chair or speak at the meeting, and finally juggles his schedule to see how many meetings he can reasonably hope to attend. Those he cannot cover must not be ignored. Usually, he arranges with someone at the meeting to telephone him afterward with the details of what happened.

The labor reporter also makes his rounds. He visits union locals, talks to the officers and the rank-and-file, phones those he cannot get to in person, and makes the rounds of management people involved in current labor stories. In a large city, with hundreds of unions and perhaps three or four strikes going on at one time, keeping track of developments is not easy. In addition, the labor reporter must also keep posted on any legislation affecting labor unions that might be brought before city, state, or provincial governments. He must keep in touch with lobbyists employed by the unions or by management to support passage of favored laws, and be able to do an "instant interpretation" story if national legislation or any event in the nation's capital has a bearing on local union affairs.

If the beat reporter is fortunate, the daily rounds are over and the information needed to write a story is gathered two or three hours before deadline. This gives the journalist a chance to go back to the paper, sit down at the typewriter, and write the stories he has gathered.

Often, however, fortune does not smile. City Council may not vote on a crucial resolution or the bargainers in union/management negotiations may not reach agreement until only minutes before deadline. The reporter, notebook in hand, must dash to the telephone and call the paper, where a copy editor seated at a typewriter and wearing earphones is ready to take the story by dictation. The reporter must compose the story on the spot, off the top of his head, as he speaks into the phone.

If, in the rush to make the deadline, he misspells a name, mixes up a quote, or forgets an important detail, he will be blamed just as harshly as if he had spent the entire day carefully composing and typing his article in the comfort of the newsroom.

Sports reporters are especially pressed for time and conscious of deadlines. They are only too well aware that the sports section is one of the main selling features of a newspaper, and late or outdated sports news is the last thing fans want to read. The final results, whether of a baseball or hockey game or of the fourth race at the local track, are what people want to know.

Sports writers, of course, become adept at the "play-by-play," recounting the progress of a game or a boxing match as it proceeds, inning by inning or round by round. In this way, by the time the final result is known three-quarters of the story is already written. All the writer has to do is go back, "put a lead on it" stating in a colorful way how the match came out, and then tack on the play-by-play. A few locker-room quotes from the principal players and the story is "in the can."

Unfortunately, a baseball game that goes into 12 innings, a basketball game in sudden death overtime, or a riot at a prize fight don't always finish on time. Sometimes the last detail cannot be had until the hands of the clock have already spelled doom for that day's sports coverage. All the sports reporter can do is grind his teeth. The next morning, fans will be reading a rival paper's account.

Editorial Writers

Only rarely faced with such frustrations are those who write the editorials, or opinion articles, which appear on the editorial page of every newspaper. These articles, which express the official view of the newspaper (often synonymous with the opinion of its publisher) on the issues of the day, are generally written a day or two before they appear and most often deal with news events that have already taken place. The editorial writer is commenting upon events, not reporting them as they happen, and has more time at his disposal.

On a large daily, there may be three or four editorial writers, one of whom is the chief and usually has the title Editor of the Editorial Page. Possible topics on which editorials might be written are suggested by the news columns of the paper itself, by the reading and discussion of individual editorial writers, or—only too frequently—by the publisher. Each morning the editorial writers meet with the publisher, and several topics are discussed, together with the viewpoint the majority of the group think the paper should express on each topic. Finally, two or three topics are chosen, and each writer is assigned one of them.

The writer then spends several hours composing an editorial on his subject, sometimes, though not always, making phone calls to people involved with the subject and pumping them for details just like an ordinary reporter. The completed editorial is handed in to the Editorial Page Editor, who may make changes, and then on to the publisher, who must give final approval before it can appear in the paper. On some newspapers the publisher allows majority rule to hold sway. If the majority of his editorial writers agree on an opinion, he goes along. At other papers, the publisher is a majority of one, the only majority, and only those opinions that agree with his personal prejudices get into print. Being an editorial writer on such a paper can be very frustrating, especially if the writer cares about his own beliefs and they run contrary to those of his boss.

Most editorials appear unsigned, and hence those who write them remain unknown to the public. In this way the authors of some of the best journalistic writing are never recognized. But, by the same token, those who had to watch helplessly as the publisher tore an editorial apart and changed its meaning entirely are at least saved the embarrassment of having their name appear on something they never intended to be taken as their own opinion.

The Rim

The real core of any newspaper operation is its "rim," that is, the crew of copy editors, headline writers, and makeup editors who sit around the rim of the two main copy desks: the city desk and the news desk (also called the wire desk). Almost all of these editors are veterans with several years' reporting experience, chosen on the basis of writing skill, news judgment, and the ability to withstand intense deadline pressure. They are generally better paid than even experienced reporters. The quality of a newspaper stands or falls on the quality of its rim.

The city desk, run by the city editor and an assistant, handles all articles dealing with local city stories. The news desk, run by the news or wire editor, handles state, national, and international stories, most of which come in from the various wire services over teleprinters or computer terminals in the paper's wire room. Together, the city and news desks usually fill at least 60 percent of the column space available in a daily newspaper.

Reporters may hand typewritten stories in at the desk, putting them in a wire basket traditionally called "the bucket," or, if the newspaper has installed computer equipment, they may file stories directly in the computer's memory by typing them on the video display terminal keyboard. Copy editors on the rim pull stories "out of the bucket" to edit, or call them up electronically on their own VDT screens.

Usually the city editors and news editors read through the day's

An editor uses a video display terminal to edit copy (photo by Thomas Pawlick).

"budget" or "schedule" of stories as soon as they arrive at work. The "sked," as it is often called, is made up by the assignment editor and lists all the stories that have been assigned that day or that are expected to arrive over the wires. As the stories are filed by the reporters or rapped out on the teleprinters, the city and news editors read them over and then hand them out to individual copy editors to "work." The editor who "deals" out stories is said to be "in the slot," and the man or woman working on a story is said to be "putting it through the magic machine."

Sometimes a great deal of magic is called for. Some reporters, although perfectly competent at gathering facts, are unable to write them down in a way that will pique a reader's interest. Their work, though accurate, is dull and boring. Others are colorful, flashy stylists but rather thin on such details as names, dates, amounts of money, addresses, ages, and so forth. Some are outright unreliable, others try to slant their stories to favor a particular side in a controversy, and still others are unable to spell.

The copy editor's job is to correct all that, to fill in all the blanks in a story, remove any bias, check all the facts, correct the spelling errors, and, last but not least, make the story interesting enough so that readers will want to read it. If a story is well written but too long, the copy editor must cut it down without changing its meaning or destroying its inherent interest.

At most dailies, the copy editor also writes a headline for each story he or she edits. The length and number of lines in each headline is usually decided by the slot man or the makeup editor, and the copy editor must write the head as requested. Sometimes it takes as long to write a good head as it does to edit or rewrite the whole story. Head writing is, in many ways, like an elaborate game of Scrabble.

Head orders are given out in a sort of code. For example, the slot man may tell an editor: "Give me a two, thirty-six once on crash, with a twenty-four kicker." This means the copy editor is to write a two-column wide headline, in 36-point type, one line deep, and with an introductory line above it in 24-point type. (A point, equal to 1/ 72 of an inch, is the measurement of height used to describe letters set in type.) The headline is to go with a story referred to as "crash" because it reports an air crash.

Writing a head that adequately describes or sums up a story, yet still fits the narrow space available for it, is no easy task. If there is room in a headline for only 19 characters, a 20-character head will be useless. "AIR CRASH KILLS FIV" rather than "AIR CRASH KILLS FIVE" is not acceptable.

A copy editor with a knack for writing lively heads that fit is worth his weight in gold to a paper. One such is veteran deskman Kevin Boland, who has worked the rim on papers from Mexico City to Montreal and points in between. So adept has he become at writing heads that he can rattle them off aloud to other deskers whenever they get stuck.

Some papers, like the Chicago *Sun-Times,* are known for their strong desk contingent, the presence of which has saved more than one mediocre reporter from looking like a fool. Others have weak desks.

At some papers a separate makeup editor actually lays out the newspaper's pages each day; at others individual copy editors are given responsibility for laying out one or two pages each per shift. The pages are diagrammed on outlines called "dummies."

Like headline writing, page layout is a specialized skill that takes talent and practice to master. The best layout men are highly skilled craftsmen and can command substantial salaries. Their ability to "dummy" a page quickly, efficiently, and artistically is not a common one.

The editors who work the rim generally stick together. A camaraderie forms among them, born of the shared daily adversity of facing deadlines and taking flack from reporters and upper-echelon editors alike. The copy editor, cutting and chopping up stories, is not generally loved by the reporters whose stories he rewrites. Often he must cut and chop reportorial egos along with the copy.

Nor is the deskman always at peace with his superiors. Some city and news editors, if they know their jobs and are willing to sit down and work a story alongside the other desk staff, become a respected part of the close-knit rim group. Other are outsiders, looked on as "the boss" and refused confidence. The rim is a kind of club, to which admission is sometimes difficult. Being part of it is always an honor.

The Columnist

Becoming a columnist may be looked upon as a blessing or a curse and is usually a mixture of both.

The blessings are fairly obvious. A columnist is paid more money than an ordinary reporter, is permitted to include more of his own personal opinion in his writing than he could put in a straight news account, and, finally, may become a sort of local celebrity—a star upon the stage of his paper's circulation area. He develops fans, people who may actually buy the paper just because his column is in it. It is more difficult for the publisher to fire him (or her) than to fire a mere reporter slogging along on a beat.

The curse side of the columnist's life is less obvious. Usually it doesn't become apparent until the columnist has been at it for a month or so and has had time for the first enthusiasm of suddenly being freed from a beat to wear off. The curse of being a columnist usually makes its appearance the first time the writer is stuck for something to write about.

It is worst for the daily columnist, who must come up with something fresh, sprightly, and interesting to say every single day of the year. Needless to say, no one really feels fresh, sprightly, and interesting every day of the year, and writing as if you do can become a terrible chore. The rate at which daily columnists quit writing their column and beg to be put back on a beat is prodigious. It is a game in which only the strong-minded survive.

Those who do survive, however, frequently contribute some of the best writing found, not only in journalism, but in all of literature. The famed Irish columnist Brian O'Nolan, who wrote a column in the *Irish Times* under the pen name of Myles na Gopaleen, is an example. His work, among the best comic writing ever produced, has been gathered in several collections and is ranked among the classics.

Other Specialties

There are many other specialties to choose from in newspaper writing and broadcasting. Both newspapers and broadcast stations, for example, usually have literary, musical, or motion picture critics on staff whose job it is to review books, concerts, and films. Sometimes these jobs are filled by local experts, working part time, sometimes by full-time staff writers with a background in the area they cover.

For instance, many newspapers ask the literature professors at local universities to write book reviews for them on a free-lance basis. Some do the same with music professors. Other newspapers hire full-time writers who have a background in the subject, such as a degree in music or drama. Others just assign an ordinary reporter who shows signs of having basic intelligence and count on the reporter to learn about the subject as he goes.

Sometimes the latter way is best. With no preconceived notions in his head, looking at art with the same viewpoint as his reading public, a neophyte reviewer may give very accurate reviews of artistic events. Sometimes, however, this sort of reviewer is a disaster. Such is the case with one motion picture/music reviewer in a major eastern city. The writer has no background in either subject except what he has picked up since being assigned to the beat. In addition, he happens to be a bit of a neurotic, who uses the column to boost his own ego.

Woe betide the musician or budding actor who fails to show this writer the exaggerated respect he thinks is due him. No matter how well they play or act, his column will tear their performance to shreds. One musician got this treatment without ever understanding why. He had never met the reviewer and did not know what he looked like. When he entered a room in which the reviewer was seated, he did not bow toward him as others had when they entered. The result was that his performance was labeled "incompetent." The adjective would apply more truthfully to the reviewer who uses his public trust in such a petty way.

Another specialty that has gained a steadily increasing importance in the decades since the end of World War II is that of science writing.

The discoveries made in science in this century, from the development of atomic energy to the ability to transplant human hearts, have had and will have a profound effect on the way people live. If the public is to make informed choices as to how the powers given us by science should be used, they must understand what those powers are and what are the choices. Writers who can interpret science subjects clearly and interestingly in layman's language have a major part to play in fostering such understanding.

Unfortunately, there are not enough persons with a good science background willing to consider science writing as a career. The field is wide open, and too often the vacuum is filled by writers who really do not understand their subjects. In future, this specialty is likely to become more and more prominent.

Whatever specialty a newcomer to journalism aims for, it will remain no more than an idle daydream if the cub fails to survive and profit from his first reporting job. The apprentice's life is no bed of roses.

CHAPTER VIII

Continuing Your Education

The student was clearly annoyed and showed it. He was also cutting his own throat but didn't seem to know it.

"This is the third night this week I've been told to work overtime without getting overtime pay," he told the features editor. "I think that's unfair. This paper is just using the students who come to work here as cheap labor. We're a bunch of coolies to be taken advantage of!"

The young man, one of six journalism students chosen to spend a summer working as reporters at a large metropolitan daily paper, was right. Of course the students were being used as cheap labor. From the paper's point of view, that was the only advantage in hiring them. They were inexperienced, bound to make bloopers and cause the editors extra work, but they had the saving grace of coming cheap—by the half dozen. They could be used to plug temporary gaps left by regular staff members on vacation, and the trade-off was basically a fair one. In return for their cheap labor, the students got priceless experience— the kind of experience they couldn't get any other way.

To complain because he wasn't getting time and a half for overtime work under this agreement was, in the young student's case, biting the hand that fed him. Unfortunately, he had made doing so a habit. His attitude during his summer stint was so poor that he stood no chance at all of getting full-time work later.

The poor fellow had a bad case of ego. He had earned very high grades at the university and shown a marked flair for writing. His teachers had encouraged him with praise, and it had gone to his head. He thought he was born to be the Star Reporter.

Perhaps he might have had the potential to become a great journalist, but to assume he already had done so at the start of his career was rushing things. He hadn't paid his dues yet, and his attitude rankled with the older, experienced people on staff. When copy editors, some of whom had twenty years' experience under their belts, rewrote his stories, he would come in the next day livid with annoyance, demanding to know why *his* copy had been changed. One day, when a copy editor told him to go stick his head under a faucet, he made the mistake of going over the copy editor's head and complaining to the city editor.

From then on, it was only a question of time before he got his walking papers. His revolt at working overtime was only the last straw. The editors decided that he would never, under any circumstances, be hired full time and that as soon as an excuse could be found to pass him back to the school that had lent him, they would be only too glad to let him go. His references, if he ever dared to ask for any from that paper, would have been dismal. In short, he did everything a cub reporter should not do.

No matter how great a young writer's raw talent may be, it is still raw talent, untrained and untried. In order to learn how to use it well, to his own and the profession's advantage, he or she must be willing to listen and to learn, to take a little ribbing when it comes and admit good-humoredly that the old-timers in the newsroom may have something worthwhile to teach.

In the days before cold type (photo-typesetting) became the rule, cub reporters were invariably the butt of endless jokes, not only by the newsroom staff, but by the printers as well. They were told to "go out in the back shop and help catch the type pigs," or asked to bend over a freshly inked page form and "look at the typelice." The "pigs" were bars of lead, which were melted down and used in Linotypes to make hot lead type. The "typelice" were specks of black printer's ink, which would pepper the unsuspecting cub's face when a grinning printer suddenly tightened the page form, causing the ink on it to spatter upward.

The pigs and typelice have gone the way of hot lead on most major dailies, but the good-natured ribbing of the cub will probably never cease. It is a kind of initiation to the club, a way to break the ice, and a small test of a new reporter's character and friendliness. No harm is meant by it.

Indeed, most experienced newsmen are eager to help a newcomer to the business. Their willingness stems partly from the fact that teaching someone the ropes is an "ego trip" for the teacher. After all, being

View of a typical composing room as staff members put page one together at the pasteup board (photo by Thomas Pawlick).

The main computer that runs the typesetting and printing operations of a modern daily newspaper (photo by Thomas Pawlick).

able to instruct somebody implies that the teacher knows something. It is a form of self-flattery. But that isn't all that's involved. A good part of the eagerness to help is based on simple concern for the underdog. A greenhorn in any job is automatically the underdog.

Having an oversized ego and a know-it-all attitude won't help a cub change this status. It won't even help an experienced reporter who actually has a few past accomplishments to boast about.

One feature writer at a major metro daily had won several awards for his writing and was recognized as an able reporter, but he let it go to his head. He became an arrogant prima donna, and gradually even those who had admired his work came to dislike him.

One afternoon a harassed assignment editor with no free bodies available asked this man, as a personal favor, to write up a batch of obituary stories for the late edition. Ordinarily, this job would be done by a cub or a desk man, but none were free. The assignment editor was asking the "star" to give him a hand in an emergency.

"What!" screamed the indignant feature writer. "Me? Write obits? What the hell is this!" He stormed and ranted for ten minutes about how great an insult such a request was, ending his tirade by refusing outright to "do one damn dead-o for this paper!" (A dead-o is slang for an obituary). The busy copy editors around the rim, who had witnessed the scene, made a mental note then and there that they would write the obit on the star feature writer's career. His future at that paper was "dead-o." Not only had he refused an assignment, proven himself an egotistical boor, and interrupted everyone else's work with his shouting, but he had defied and annoyed the assignment editor, one of the rim's "own" people.

In less than a year the feature writer resigned. The editors saw to it that he received only the dullest, most unimportant stories to cover, and his writing—once it had gone through the rim for editing—was thoroughly dead by the time it saw print. His by-line rarely, if ever, appeared on a page, and he himself got the most silent of silent treatments from the deskmen.

It was a ruthless way to teach a lesson, but it is likely that the writer in question, wherever he is presently employed, is considerably more humble about his status on the job and more helpful toward his fellow workers.

Building Contacts

A new reporter, particularly if his first job is on a paper outside of his home town, is hampered by a lack of knowledge of the community and by a lack of "contacts," of people who can provide information, advice, and expertise on various subjects or help in getting a job done. Contacts also include a reporter's personal network of tipsters and story sources, which a cub has yet to develop.

Realizing the difficulty of the situation, most employers try to help a cub break in by sending him on fairly easy assignments at first, covering routine press conferences, Rotary or Lions Club meetings, and other functions where his lack of knowledge won't be too constricting. In between these assignments, the cub can begin to familiarize himself with the city, with the background of current news stories, and with the paper's staff.

For backgrounding and a knowledge of the community, the clip file or morgue is the best place to start. There a reporter can read through back issues of the paper and see how each story began. He may, for example, wonder why the assault trial of Jack Klutz was reported on page one. A glance through earlier issues may reveal that Jack Klutz is no ordinary brawler, but a well-known labor leader who got into a fight while walking the picket line in a bitter, six-month strike that still divides the community. Reading further back, he may discover that a similar strike took place five years ago and that the city's mayor won the last election because he supported the strikers. Thus Jack Klutz's trial becomes more than an assault case. It becomes a political event, worthy of page one coverage.

Talking to other staff members also serves to background a new reporter and provides the cub with his first professional contacts. A writer for the finance or business page, for example, can be of immense value in helping a cub on general assignment handle a story dealing with business. The city hall reporter can help on stories involving the local politicos, and the crime reporter can help on police stories. If any of these people volunteer aid or information, a cub should grab it and thank them.

Beat reporters are especially happy to help if a cub on general assignment is relieving them of extra work by doing a story they didn't have time to do themselves. The city hall reporter, for example, may be busy with an important council meeting and not have time to do an interview with the head of a local neighborhood improvement association. He might ask the assignment editor to give the story to someone else, and thus the cub can inherit it.

In such cases the regular beat person is usually quite willing to provide the cub with phone numbers, a quick summation of the personality and reputation of the person to be interviewed, and a hint or two about what kind of story the interview will likely produce.

Phone numbers, especially, are valuable. Often the phone numbers of city officials, labor union officers, and the upper managers of large companies are not listed in the phone book. The only way to obtain these confidential numbers is to get them from their owners or from a reporter who already has them.

The person the cub is sent to interview may become another contact. The head of a neighborhood association may be knowledgeable about the doings of an alderman or city council member, including not-so-legal doings. Perhaps the association member will become a tipster, telling the reporter about a crooked sewer contract or a bribe.

A reporter on a story never knows when one of the people he or she meets may turn out to be a valuable source, if not immediately, then perhaps on some future occasion.

One young reporter was sent out to do a series of interviews with two policewomen in the sheriff's department, intending to write a color story on "A day in the life of a policewoman." The reporter made friends with the two officers, and both were pleased with his handling of the initial story. Neither woman had mentioned it during these early interviews, but they were working on a mass-murder investigation involving the killing of several female students at a nearby university. One morning the reporter was riding in a squad car with one of the policewomen when a call came over the radio to help pick up a suspect. It was the mass murderer. "We're about to arrest the co-ed killer, want to come along?" the officer asked the reporter. Obviously, he did.

His subsequent story on the arrest made page one and scored a "national beat," that is, it was the first story on an event of national interest. If he had not made the initial contact with the policewomen and gained their trust, he would never have had a shot at the second story.

Perhaps the ultimate example of the value of contacts was provided by Bob Woodward and Carl Bernstein, the Washington *Post* reporters whose stories on the break-in at Democratic Party headquarters in the Watergate building in Washington led eventually to the exposure and resignation of President Nixon and won the Pulitzer Prize. They owed their reporting success to "inside" government contacts—especially the source they called Deep Throat.

Sometimes taking a person to lunch, buying them a beer, or simply being friendly to them can lead to the special relationship that develops between reporters and their "informed sources."

News Sense

In addition to being open-minded and developing contacts, a new reporter should also be sharpening his or her "news sense."

News sense is a subtle, complex quality and involves much more than the simple instinct that enables a reporter to recognize an event as newsworthy. It involves the ability to spot phony stories and setups, to differentiate between legitimate announcements and mere publicity or promotional blather, to sense when a source is trying to manipulate the reporter and when a person being interviewed is lying or shading the truth.

News sense, in other words, is a synonym for professional judgment. The extent to which a reporter develops and exhibits such judgment governs in large measure how far he advances in his chosen field. A reporter with "solid news sense" would not have been fooled by the woman with the retarded child mentioned in Chapter II, nor by others who try to use newspaper publicity for their own ends. Such persons are legion, and the ends they have in mind are equally numerous. They range from promoters pushing manufactured products to agents selling rock bands.

A well-run public relations firm's account executives spend most of their working day trying to figure out ways to get reporters to write stories about their clients. They study the reporters' personalities, foibles, and hobbies and will contort a fact or statement wildly to pique the reporter's interest or play up to an editor. It is not always simple to see through them.

News sense is not learned in a classroom or passed on by textbooks. It can only be acquired through personal experience, and some beginners find the acquisition rather rough. As a rule of thumb, most reporters get burned by a phony at least once in their first year on the job. The experience usually makes them wary, which is a valuable attribute in a journalist.

Honing Your Style

Just after news sense in order of importance among the on-the-job subjects to be absorbed by a cub comes writing style. It is true that the copy editors on the rim can put even the most poorly written story into shape for publication, but both they and the readers will be getting a break if each reporter develops a "clean" writing style of his own.

Nothing is more pleasing to a copy editor working on deadline than to be handed a story to edit and discover that it doesn't need editing, that the reporter wrote well enough to put the article directly into print: "No muss, no fuss, just plain English," as the rim people say.

One such reporter was the education writer mentioned in Chapter V who had taught himself to type with one finger. Despite his odd typing style, his stories were models of clarity, logic, and objectivity. Often the slotman would deal one of his stories out to whichever copy editor had been the busiest on a given shift. It was like offering the harassed editor a coffee break. All he had to do was make "hooks" where paragraphs started and write a headline. The story required no editing.

Needless to say, those who worked the rim had nothing but good to say about the education reporter. He was their darling and was eventually promoted to a desk position himself, at higher pay.

This particular reporter was not a colorful stylist or feature writer, nor was he particularly artistic. He was a beat man, but his writing was so easy to read that it needed no improvement. Every cub should strive to develop a straight news writing style that is clear and unambiguous. Copy editors call this "clean writing." Even those who plan on becoming feature writers and who have a literary bent should develop a clean news style *in addition* to their feature style. The Associated Press wire stores are good models to follow in trying to develop a good straight news style. Wire copy is as clear and plain as the proverbial pikestaff and very easy to edit.

The AP's rewrite people pride themselves on being able to remove excess verbiage from stories, "chopping" whole columns from daily newspapers into one or two paragraphs of wire copy. They might, for example, take the following sentence: "Upon consultation with several advisers, Mayor Clampett announced, he had come to a decision on the zoning request." Rewritten by the AP, it would come out: "Following talks with advisers, Mayor Clampett agreed to rule on the zone request." The first sentence took 18 words to complete, the second 13 words. Carried through the length of a story, this kind of condensing produces startling space saving.

Feature Styles

As for feature styles, they are as varied and numerous as the feature writers who employ them. Unlike straight news copy, feature styles bear the mark of their authors. No two are exactly alike, and the only limits to the amount of ingenuity and originality they reflect are the patience of the paper's editors and the comprehension of its readership. Particularly since the 1960's, when the so-called New Journalism made its appearance, feature techniques have come to include nearly every literary device imaginable.

Tom Wolfe, for example, began a feature story describing the Las Vegas gambling subculture with a full paragraph containing the same word, repeated over and over: "Hernia, hernia, hernia, hernia, hernia . . ." The sound produced by reading this paragraph aloud rapidly, Wolfe noted, was identical to the sound produced in a casino by the crowd of gamblers, croupiers, and spectators all talking at once. The word hernia was also a metaphor for the psychological effect the gambling mania had on its victims—that is, it produced a mental hernia.

Another writer, this one a columnist sent to cover a political speech by a local Congressman, found the speech idiotic. Even by the normal standards of political speeches, it was inane, and the columnist was disgusted. He came back to the paper, slipped a page into his typewriter, and began: "A black-tie, $100-a-plate dinner for Congressman John Doe featured a long, carefully prepared speech by the Republican legislator on the nuclear question. The Congressman said . . . ." The rest of the column, five inches of newspaper space, was left blank.

Another feature writer, the late Detroit *News* sports columnist Doc Greene, specialized in writing that presented an unorthodox point of view. Whereas other sports writers concentrated on the boxers in the ring at a prize fight, Greene watched the bettors and bookies in the audience, recording their ups and downs along with the boxers'. His theory was that any contest between living things that attracted spectators was a sport. He once devoted a column to the epic battle between two Siamese fighting fish in a pet shop aquarium and the reaction of the men who had bet cash on the outcome. The column was a play-by-play, describing each watery lunge and brush of fins as if it were a heavyweight title match.

Such is the stuff of modern feature writing.

Reading the work of other writers is a good way for a cub to open his mind to the possibilities of the written word and to learn from the mistakes and successes of the best professionals.

Among the best current writers of newspaper and magazine feature articles are Tom Wolfe, Jimmy Breslin, Mike Royko, and Hunter Thompson. Earlier masters of the form included Ernest Hemingway, George Ade, Flann O'Brien, and George Orwell.

As a glance at these names makes plain, many of the best newspaper and magazine writers have gone on to become major figures in English literature. Writers who got their start in the newsroom, writing columns or feature stories, also include Mark Twain, Bret Harte, and Carl Sandburg.

Simply because a cub reporter has finished school—whether the course was at a university or in the school of hard knocks—and gotten a newspaper job doesn't mean his education is complete. Studying human nature, developing news sense, learning about a community, cultivating sources, perfecting both straight news and feature writing styles are steps in a continuing education that goes on throughout a journalist's career.

If a reporter develops a specialty, such as government reporting or science writing, he must plan on constantly adding to his knowledge of the subject area. Science writers subscribe to stacks of scientific journals and read them all; government reporters are continually discussing and reflecting upon political issues, theories, and personalities. It is a process that never stops, and never ought to stop.

The day a journalist's education is complete, he will publish his last story. Afterward, there will be nothing to report, because that journalist will be dead.

CHAPTER IX

Many and Various

Newspapers and broadcast stations, like the people who run them, have personalities. Some are stuffy and formal, some are relaxed and friendly, and some are flashy and irresponsible. They exhibit regional differences as well as differences of wealth, class, and political persuasion.

A job-hunter hoping to make a good impression on a prospective employer would be wise to take the personality of the employer's station or paper into consideration. It is a reflection of the way management thinks, or more accurately, how management believes its readers or listeners think.

The editors of the New York *Times,* for example, believe their readers are the business, academic, and political leaders of the United States and that the *Times* is the "newspaper of record" for the country. As a consequence, they produce a thick, weighty tome (the Sunday *Times* is probably the bulkiest paper in the nation, heavy enough to give its carriers a hernia), crammed with detail and ponderous pronouncements. The *Times* does, of course, contain excellent, well-researched articles and in the past has produced some of the greatest reporting in American history.

Unfortunately, it is sometimes a bit too impressed with its own past greatness and reputation and tends to produce stilted, somewhat pompous writing. Its layout and type style have been deliberately kept old-fashioned as a gesture to tradition, making the typical *Times* front page displeasing to the eye and difficult to read.

Obviously, a newspaper as pretentious as the *Times* would never consider hiring a beginner, nor, for that matter, would it be likely to hire a stylistic innovator like Tom Wolfe.

The New York *Herald Tribune,* now defunct, was precisely the opposite. It had a sense of adventure. Not only did it give Wolfe his start, but it hired and launched Jimmy Breslin, Dick Schaap, and a lineup of other first-class originals. Its Sunday pictorial magazine, *New York,* eventually became the present-day *New York* magazine after the paper itself had folded. At the *Tribune,* innovation and originality were at a premium, along with a certain degree of sophistication.

Still another personality is evident at the *Daily News,* which proclaims itself "New York's picture newspaper." The *News* is a blunt, tabloid-sized daily with a circulation in excess of two million readers nationally and a conservative political philosophy. It aims its short, simple articles at a largely blue-collar readership and specializes in projecting a "big-city tough guy with a heart of gold" image. A typical headline once summed up a New York-Washington financial conflict in five words: "Ford to City: Drop Dead!"

Although they all originated in the same city, each of these papers developed its own character and its own readership. Similar differences between papers are found in Chicago, Detroit, and Toronto. In Toronto, *The Star* and *The Globe and Mail* both have pretentions to be Canada's national newspaper of record, and the now-defunct Toronto *Telegram* and the relatively new tabloid Toronto *Sun* fill positions vaguely like those of the *Herald Tribune* and *Daily News,* respectively.

The regional and national differences between newspapers are also significant. Papers in the southern states tend to be more conservative politically than those in the North and, probably because their pay scales are so much lower, attract fewer talented writers. Papers in Canada's Maritime provinces are similarly handicapped as against the dailies of central Canada.

In the United States, where free speech and a free press are guaranteed in writing in the nation's constitution, the courts are reluctant to interpret libel laws too strictly for fear of denying a constitutionally assured right. In Canada, where a free press is traditional but not protected by a written constitution, libel laws are much more restrictive—and judges much harsher—than in the U.S. The result is that Canadian papers are less likely to produce exposés or investigative journalism than their American counterparts. The risk of being successfully sued by someone mentioned in such an article, and harshly punished by the courts, is too great.

Newspapers are also heavily influenced by the presence of large blocs of minority, ethnic, or religious group readers among their audiences. A newspaper in Salt Lake City, Utah, inevitably reflects the overwhelming presence of the Mormon Church in the city, just as a Boston paper is indirectly affected by the Irish and a paper in Corpus Christi, Texas, by the Spanish-speaking Chicanos of that region.

Any large group of readers with similar views is bound to have an effect on a paper, even if the effect is felt only in the Letters to the Editor column. An upstate daily with a large farm audience sees the world differently from a daily in a factory town whose readers are union men. The presence of a farm audience tends to create pressure in favor of a conservative, Republican Party viewpoint, whereas that of a union readership favors liberal, Democratic Party views.

Union influence may be felt internally, as well as externally, if the staff of the newspaper itself is unionized.

Newspaper Unions

The printers and pressmen at most North American dailies are union members, the printers most often belonging to the International Typographical Union (ITU).

Although the editorial employees of many dailies are also organized, belonging either to the ITU or the North American Newspaper Guild, reporters and photographers have traditionally been reluctant to join unions. In part, their reluctance was due to mere snobbery. Reporters particularly liked to regard themselves as members of a professional group, like lawyers or doctors, and looked upon union membership as a step down in the social scale. Only when they realized that the less pretentious people in the back shop were making higher salaries than some reporters did many newsmen and women change their tune.

Not all of the traditional editorial aversion to union membership was based on snobbery, however. A good deal of it stemmed from a legitimate concern over newspaper standards. The idea that a reporter might be promoted or given raises not on the basis of ability, enterprise in getting the news, or the originality of his writing, but merely according to the number of months or years he had worked for the paper—the seniority principle—was abhorrent to many. So was the prospect of a closed shop, in which only union members could write for a newspaper. This automatically would exclude free-lance writers who did not work for the paper full time and hence were not members of the bargaining unit.

Many reporters supplement their income by writing free-lance articles for noncompeting publications, and most are aware that some free lancers are among the best journalists writing today. Professional fairness makes them oppose the possibility of rejecting a great story because its author isn't on the dues check-off list.

An editorial bargaining unit can, of course, write contracts that take such concerns into consideration. The members of a Newspaper Guild unit might stipulate that free-lancing is permitted at their paper and that promotions should be based at least 50 percent on merit. A good union should be run on a democratic basis, and its officers ought to seek only what their members tell them to go after. In reality, however, things are rarely so simple.

Journalists, like those in other lines of work, tend to be lazy about taking on extra loads. The most able and ambitious among them are often so intent on doing their reporting jobs well that they don't want to take time away from them. Such tasks as going to union meetings, canvassing members, or spending hours arguing bread-and-butter issues with management or their co-workers are regarded as unwelcome interruptions or annoying chores. It is easier not to go to meetings and to leave the haggling to somebody else.

Cliques form. A small group may take over direction of the local and set its policy in a vacuum, by default. Sometimes, when apathy develops among the rank and file, management itself takes over. The members of one wire service unit, for example, were shocked when the chairman of their bargaining unit, during a strike for which he had voted, became the first to cross the picket line and return to work. Not long afterward they found out why he had done it when he was promoted to news editor. The promotion was management's payoff for helping to break the strike.

As one columnist noted during an argument with his co-workers prior to an organizational vote at a large daily: "In principle, I'm for bringing in the union, but in practice I think we'd be opening up a can of worms."

As the years go on and inflation continues to drive up the cost of living, however, more and more editorial employees are voting to join a union. Some vote for Guild membership and some bring in the ITU, but the basic motive for all is higher pay and greater job security. The highest principles and most stringently conservative standards tend to give way when jobs and paychecks are at stake.

At the Detroit *News,* which for years had kept the union out of its editorial department by maintaining its salary levels at or above those of the unionized Detroit *Free Press,* employees finally voted to organize when management, in the early 1970's, indulged in an unexpectedly ruthless mass layoff of reporters and editors. A similar scenario was played out at the Montreal *Gazette* when a new management team imported from Toronto created such insecurity among staff members that they voted in 1977 to join the Guild.

Perhaps in future it will be as rare to find a paper whose reporters and photographers are not union members as it is now to find one whose printers have not been organized.

Things to Come

Predicting the future is always a chancy project, and nowhere more so than in the changeable field of journalism, prone to fads and fancies and the vagaries of the economy. Seen through the perspective of several decades, however, certain patterns emerge, trends that may indicate where the industry is heading.

The most obvious trend, particularly since World War II, has been toward corporate chain ownership of newspapers and the development of local newspaper monopolies. At the beginning of this century, many large North American cities boasted a dozen or more daily papers, all battling fiercely for survival in the crowded marketplace. Their number and diversity provided outlets for a wide variety of opinions.

But the rising costs of production and distribution, of newsprint, labor, mailing, and machinery and equipment, inevitably reduced their numbers. As late as 1960 there were still eight daily newspapers in New York City and five in Chicago. Today there are only three dailies left in New York and three (including the *Wall Street Journal* Midwest edition) in Chicago. Whereas most dailies were once independently owned by local investors, by 1967 half of the daily papers in the United States were chain-owned, and nine out of ten of all daily papers were monopolies, that is, papers with no competition in the cities in which they were published. By 1979 fully 97 percent of the 1,544 American cities with daily papers were one-paper towns, and three out of every four newspaper readers were reading a paper owned by a corporate chain.

Even in large cities with more than one daily, competition has been reduced to a minimum. Usually, one of the two remaining dailies is a morning paper and the other an evening one. They serve slightly different audiences and carry slightly different kinds of advertising. More and more often, the managers of such theoretically rival papers have agreements to share production facilities, bargain jointly with their unions, and even share the costs of syndicate subscriptions. In Minneapolis, for example, the morning *Tribune* and the evening *Star* maintain separate editorial staffs and separate names in their mastheads, but both are owned by the same company, the Minneapolis Star and Tribune Company, and they share the same business staff.

In Kansas City, Missouri, the morning *Times* and evening *Star* are both owned by the Kansas City Star Company and have partially merged their staffs. In Vancouver, British Columbia, the *Province* and *Sun* share production facilities. The trend is evident everywhere: daily newspaper ownership is becoming concentrated in fewer and fewer hands. The Gannett Company chain in 1979 owned 77 newspapers in 30 U.S. states. The publishing empire of the Canadian-born Lord Thomson of Fleet included more than 50 American newspapers, in addition to the chain's British and Canadian holdings.

The dwindling number of daily newspapers and the increasing concentration of their ownership have led many observers to fear that free speech could be stifled. Indeed, some critics charge that it already is, that only those views which correspond with those of the managers of the corporate news chains are likely to be published. Whether such fears are exaggerated or not is open to question. It is certain, however, that corporate ownership does seem to have led to corporate blandness in the media. As *Esquire* magazine puts it: "Front pages tend to look alike, editors tend to run the same kinds of stories in the same ways to attract the same kinds of readers, and publishers tend to follow similar promotion, advertising, and circulation strategies."

Fortunately for the reading public, competition has not entirely vanished from the daily newspaper industry. Suburban papers, such as the Long Island–based *Newsday* outside New York or the *Eccentric* papers in the suburbs of Detroit, compete with urban dailies. Some cities have even witnessed the birth of new daily papers, such as the Toronto *Sun,* whose phenomenal success is in marked contrast to the death throes of the old Toronto *Telegram.* Weekly papers, such as *The Village Voice* in New York, also help to fill the gap left by the shrinking number of dailies.

Magazine Boom

If diversity appears under siege in the daily newspaper field, it is on the offensive in magazine journalism, where a whole new spectrum of publications has arisen and even the dead are coming back to life.

In the 1950's and 1960's several of the most venerable and respected general magazines—*Look, Collier's, The Saturday Evening Post,* and *Life*—went out of business. Industry observers believed magazine journalism was doomed, replaced by television. They were wrong. For every general magazine that folded, a spate of new specialty magazines was born, from *MS* to *Mother Earth News.* Readers had not stopped reading; they had simply narrowed the focus of what they wanted to read about or become part of special interest groups. Magazines responded to that change, and today they are as numerous as ever.

Even the old general magazines—including both *Life* and *The Saturday Evening Post*—have been resurrected as television viewers seek greater detail and more thoughtful interpretation of the headlines read to them over the tube. Optimism and a willingness to take risks abound in the magazine field, where such established publications as *The National Geographic* are being challenged by new arrivals such as *Geo,* and where publications such as Canada's *Harrowsmith,* started on a farmhouse kitchen table, can rise in three years to a circulation in excess of 125,000.

The vitality and growth of magazine journalism are likely to continue in the coming years.

So, for that matter, is the health of the weekly newspaper field, as phototypesetting and web offset printing processes cut labor and production costs and make it possible for more investors to enter the weekly sector.

Job Opportunities

Every profession seems to undergo periodic labor surpluses, brought on by changes in the economy or by changes in popular fashion. Whole mobs of engineers were graduated in the late 1950's and early 1960's, especially aeronautical engineers. The nation was obsessed with its technological competition with the Soviet Union—the Sputnik cra- and couldn't get enough people to build and man new rockets and aircraft. Then, only a few years later, the industry cut back. Boeing, North American Rockwell, and other companies began laying off personnel, and cities like Seattle and Cape Kennedy became ghost towns for the unemployed.

The same thing happened with teachers as the postwar "baby boom" generation grew up and left school. The universities had graduated

*A Linotype, the machine formerly used to set "hot" molten-lead
type, which has been rendered obsolete by modern phototypesetting
(photo by Thomas Pawlick).*

too many engineers and too many teachers, and they found themselves
joining the ranks of the jobless.

Similar phases strike the newspaper business. During the Watergate
scandals of the Nixon administration the press played a prominent
role and reporters like Woodward and Bernstein became folk heroes
extolled in popular motion pictures. As a result, the enrollment at journalism schools swelled. Everybody wanted to be a glamorous reporter,
toppling presidents and starring in movies. Inevitably this brought a
surplus of job-hunters into the marketplace.

The surplus, however, was temporary. Surpluses always are, and even if they were not, there is one type of job applicant who never seems to be available in surplus, namely, the hard-working, talented person who won't take "no" for an answer and won't give up. Such people will always find jobs, no matter how many others are competing for them.

Automation may throw pressmen or Linotypers out of work, but it will never replace reporters and editors for the simple reason that machines—even the most sophisticated computers—cannot observe and write. The opportunities in journalism are many and various, and always will be.

CHAPTER X

Read On . . .

Claiming to have adequately described the field of journalism in a single book would be like claiming to have given a successful one-week course in brain surgery. The subject is simply too broad for one author to do it justice. Anyone seriously interested in the possibility of making journalism a career should seek out further sources of information, both personal and printed.

When possible, interested persons should try to get the opinion of someone already working in the business, of a reporter, editor, or newscaster who would be willing to discuss the trials and satisfactions of the profession frankly, as well as to provide hints on how to break in at the local level.

As for further reading on the subject, there are so many books, magazines, and pamphlets available that picking out those of genuine worth might be a bit confusing for the uninitiated. The following bibliography, based on fifteen years of personal, practical experience, should help simplify the task:

Information on the Industry and on Writing Style

Mott, G. F. *New Survey of Journalism.* College Outline Series, Barnes & Noble, New York, 1963.

This is probably the best all-around, quick outline of the field of journalism that you can buy. It has everything in it from the history of journalism in the United States to writing an article, writing headlines, and laying out pages, as well as a good glossary of newspaper jargon. On top of all this, it's a paperback and can be bought inexpensively.

Taylor, H. B. and Scher, J. *Copy Reading and News Editing.* Prentice-Hall, Englewood Cliffs, New Jersey, 1955.

This is a hardbound basic journalism text used in many university journalism schools and available at most public libraries. It is an excellent reference book, with clear explanations of how to write articles, edit copy, lay out pages, write headlines, and perform all the nuts-and-bolts tasks in the newsroom. It goes into greater detail than the College Outline paperback and is more technical in orientation.

Cranford, Robert J. *Copy Editing Workbook.* Holt, Rinehart & Winston, New York, 1967.

This is a practical exercise book showing how to edit and lay out newspaper stories. It provides good practice and is inexpensive.

Strunk, William, Jr., and White, E. B. *The Elements of Style.* The MacMillan Co., New York, 1972.

A classic reference book on grammar and writing style, used in newsrooms everywhere. It's a pocket-sized, hardbound book and very readable.

Columbia Journalism Review, 200 Alton Place, Marion, OH 43302.

Published under the auspices of the Columbia University Graduate School of Journalism, this monthly magazine is the conscience and critic of the newspaper industry in North America, containing articles that weigh the performance, bad or good, of the media.

The Writer, 8 Arlington Street, Boston, MA 02116.

A monthly magazine containing excellent how-to articles on writing and selling stories to newspapers and magazines. Each issue contains a detailed listing of current free-lance markets and their requirements.

Writer's Digest, 9933 Alliance Road, Cincinnati, OH 45242.

A monthly magazine similar to *The Writer* but with less extensive market lists. All three of the above-mentioned magazines are carried in public libraries.

Free lance Market Lists

Aside from the magazines mentioned above, the following books give extensive market listings and are available in most public libraries:

Burack, A. S. *The Writer's Handbook.* The Writer, Inc., Boston, Massachusetts. Published yearly.

Ellinwood, Lynne, and Moser, Jo Anne. *Writer's Market.* Writer's Digest, Cincinnati, Ohio. Published yearly.

Blaufox, Janice. *LMP (Literary Market Place).* R. R. Bowker Company, New York, N.Y. Published yearly.

Brady, John. *The Writer's Yearbook.* Writer's Yearbook, Cincinnati, Ohio. Published yearly in magazine format.

Goodman, Eileen. *The Canadian Writer's Market.* McClelland & Stewart Ltd., Toronto, Canada, 1976.

The Writers and Artists Yearbook. The Writer, Inc., Boston, Massachusetts. Published yearly. Gives British and British Commonwealth markets.

Fulton, Len, and May, James Boyer. *Directory of Little Magazines and Small Presses.* Paradise, California. Published yearly. Gives list of underground, alternative, and small papers and magazines.

Gebbie, Con. *Gebbie House Magazine Directory.* House Magazine Publishing Company Inc., Sioux City, Iowa. Published yearly. Lists trade magazines and magazines published by corporations for their own employees.

Where to Look for Full-time Jobs

Editor & Publisher, 575 Lexington Avenue, New York, NY 10022.

This is unquestionably the best place to look for classified advertisements by newspapers seeking reporting staff. A weekly magazine, its classified section is avidly read by people in the business, half of whom have gotten jobs through it. Job-seekers can place their own ads in the "Positions Wanted, Editorial" section for a reasonably low fee.

Content, 91 Raglan Avenue, Toronto, Ontario, Canada M6C 2K7.

This is the Canadian equivalent of *Editor & Publisher* and also contains a classified ad section listing jobs available. You can place your own Positions Wanted ad here, too.

Editor & Publisher Yearbook. Published yearly by the same people who put out the magazine, *E&P* lists every newspaper, daily or weekly, in the world, their names, addresses, and circulation figures. For U.S. and Canadian papers, it lists the names of the key business and editorial executives to whom applicants can apply personally for jobs or information. Available in public libraries.

The Ayer Directory. Similar to the *E&P Yearbook,* but less detailed, it is also available in most public libraries.

Journalism Schools

Most school and public libraries keep reference books listing colleges and universities. Among the best such reference series are the *Barron's Guides.* There are guides to two-year and four-year schools, listing subjects taught and other information. Catalogs are also available from universities on request.

Books for Fun and Personal Enrichment

Woodward, R. and Bernstein, C. *All the President's Men.* Warner Books Inc., New York, 1975.

Written by the Washington *Post* reporters who exposed the Watergate scandal and won a Pulitzer Prize doing so, this is an excellent descriptive picture of reporters in action. A good feeling is given of how things work in a newsroom, and it's a great story besides.

Wolfe, Tom. *The Kandy Kolored Tangerine Flake Streamline Baby.* Pocket Books, New York, 1971.

An example of modern newspaper feature writing at its best, by an original (very original) writing stylist. Reading it will loosen up a person's mind as well as writing style.

Wolfe, Tom, and Johnson, E. W. *The New Journalism.* Harper & Row, Publishers, New York, 1973.

Notable especially for Wolfe's introductory essay "The Feature Game," this is an anthology of some of the best examples of present-day feature writing, including articles by Hunter Thompson, Gay Talese, and other masters of the craft.

White, W. *By-Line Ernest Hemingway.* Bantam Books, New York, 1968.

A collection of Nobel Prize-winning novelist Ernest Hemingway's best newspaper and magazine feature articles. The articles are the work of a master, study of whose work can help anyone.

Royko, M. *Slats Grobnik and Some Other Friends.* Popular Library, Toronto, 1976.

An example of humorous newspaper column writing by the Pulitzer Prize-winning Chicago columnist Mike Royko.

Shepherd, Jean. *The America of George Ade.* G. P. Putman's Sons, New York, 1961.

A collection of the "fables in slang" written as columns in the old Chicago *Record* in the 1890's by a pioneer newspaper humorist, George Ade.

O'Nolan, Kevin. *The Best of Myles.* Walker and Company, New York, 1968.

The best columns by Brian O'Nolan, whose column "The Cruiskeen Lawn" appeared in *The Irish Times* (Dublin) under the pen name Myles na Gopaleen.

Pyle, Ernie. *Last Chapter.* Henry Holt & Company, New York, 1946.

A collection of the last dispatches by America's great war correspondent, who was killed in the Pacific campaign in World War II.

Davis, Richard Harding. *The Notes of a War Correspondent.* Charles Scribner's Sons, New York, 1911. Out of print but worth searching the dusty back shelves of a library for, this is a collection of dispatches from one of the best war correspondents of the last century, a direct journalistic predecessor of Hemingway who covered the Spanish-American and Boer wars.

Lewis, Roger. *Outlaws of America.* Pelican Books, London, 1972. An introduction to and brief history of the underground press in North America and Great Britain during the 1960's and early 1970's, the height of the "Movement" years.

White, William Allen. *The Autobiography of William Allen White.* The MacMillan Company, New York, 1946. The story of the best-known weekly newspaper publisher in the United States, whose Emporia (Kansas) *Gazette* was an American institution and whose editorials were among the best ever written.

Smith, Dennis, *Report from Engine Co. 82.* Pocket Books, New York, 1973.

The true story of the life of a fireman in New York, reported by the fire fighter/journalist himself.

Franklin, Benjamin. *An Apology for Printers.* Acropolis Books Ltd., 1965. A famous essay by one of the Founding Fathers of the United States on the subject of press freedom and responsibility.

Orwell, George. *The Road to Wigan Pier.* Berkley Publishing Corporation, New York, 1961.

An excellent example of personal reportage by a great journalist who became a great novelist, this is the story of Orwell's life with the miners and industrial workers of northern England during the Great Depression of the 1930's.

Breslin, Jimmy. *Can't Anybody Here Play This Game?*

The story of the New York Mets' first wacky season as a professional baseball team, as seen through the eyes of columnist Jimmy Breslin. An unusual example of sports reporting.

Talese, Gay. *The Kingdom and the Power.*

The story of the New York *Times,* an American newspaper institution, by ex-Timesman Talese.

Five Great Newspapers

To understand the standards against which a newspaper and its reporters should be measured, an acquaintance with the best newspapers currently being published is necessary. Probably the five best-written, most authoritative and objective daily newspapers are, in order of excellence:

Le Monde (Paris, France; English edition also published).
The Times (London, England).
The Christian Science Monitor (Boston, Massachusetts; mainly for its coverage of foreign affairs).
The Wall Street Journal (New York and Chicago; for its business coverage and Page One features).
The New York Times (New York, N.Y., slipping, but still up there.)
The best examples of current magazine feature writing and in-depth journalism are probably found in *Esquire* magazine and *Harper's* magazine. Many of the most accomplished journalists writing today got their start on one or the other of these publications, and the standards of both remain consistently high. Also of exceptionally high quality is the writing in *The New Yorker,* and less consistently in *New York* magazine.

Copies of these newspapers and magazines are available at most public libraries, with the possible exception of *Le Monde* and *The Times* of London, which may sometimes be purchased at shops that sell out-of-town papers and magazines.

Appendix

A Sample Résumé

An applicant going job-hunting should have a neatly typed résumé, or curriculum vitae, to present to prospective employers along with his or her writing samples.

The résumé should include the applicant's full name and address, a list of schools attended, courses followed and diplomas, degrees, or certificates earned. It should also list all of the applicant's work experience, including companies worked for, dates employed, and the nature of the duties performed.

Finally, the résumé should give a list of personal references, preferably people who know the job-hunter's character as well as his or her work performance. Photocopies of the résumé can be sent to as many prospective employers as desired, and followed up wherever possible with a phone call and personal visit.

Following is an example of how a résumé might be organized:

NAME John Doe   *Birth Date* 2/15/51   *Height* 5′10″
Weight 160   *Address* 143 Pine Street, Baltimore, Md
Married Yes   *Children* 2   *Military Status* 3A   *Physical*
Limitations None   *Languages* German

Schools	Dates	Degrees
Edison Community College Fort Meyers, Florida	9/69 to 6/71	Associate Degree (Journalism Major)

Employment	Dates	Duties
Ajax Soap Co Baltimore, Md	9/69 to 5/70	Label stamper Shift supervisor
United Box & Bag Inc Fort Meyers, Florida	5/70 to 6/71	Public relations Copywriting

Free Lance

Articles on sports, local politics for the *Weekly Blade,* Baltimore, Md.
Stringer for *Box and Bag News,* in Baltimore.

Miscellaneous

Articles in student newspaper at Edison Community College.
Winner of 1970 Nansen Award for excellence in composition.

References

Ajax Soap Co., Jack Sudds, Plant Manager. Phone (301) 561–3334.
The Weekly Blade, Peter Sharp, Editor. Phone (301)565–7774.
Edison Community College, Alan Mosley, professor of journalism.
 Phone: (813) 736–2894.